~~WOMEN'S STUDIES~~
~~c/o EVELYN S. NEWLYN~~
~~ENGLISH DEPT., VPI&SU~~

WOMEN'S STUDIES LIBRARY
10 SANDY HALL
VIRGINIA TECH

D1786831

Women's Center
206 Washington Street
Blacksburg, VA 24061-0270
(540) 231-7806

D.H. LAWRENCE AND FEMINISM

D. H. Lawrence and Feminism

Hilary Simpson

Northern Illinois University Press
DeKalb, Illinois
1982

© 1982 Hilary Simpson
Northern Illinois University Press, DeKalb,
Illinois 60115

Library of Congress Card Number: 82-14446
ISBN 0-87580-090-4

Printed and bound in Great Britain

CONTENTS

Acknowledgements

Note on Editions Used

Introduction 13

1. The Suffragist 19

2. The Dreaming Woman 46

3. Lawrence, Feminism and the War 63

4. The Context of Lawrence's Sexual Theory 81

5. Man to Man 99

6. The Phallic Consciousness 122

7. A Literary Trespasser 143

Bibliography 164

Index 172

ACKNOWLEDGEMENTS

I am grateful to Laurence Pollinger Ltd and the Estate of Mrs Frieda Lawrence Ravagli for permission to quote from Lawrence's works; and to Pergamon Press Ltd for permission to reproduce Chapter 7, which first appeared as an article in *Women's Studies International Quarterly* in 1979.

I should also like to thank Catherine Banting for typing the manuscript and John Simpson for his valuable assistance.

NOTE ON EDITIONS USED

The following short titles are used in the notes:

Letters	*The Letters of D.H. Lawrence*: vol. 1, ed. James T. Boulton (Cambridge University Press, Cambridge, 1979); vol. 2, ed. George J. Zytaruk and James T. Boulton (1981)
Collected Letters	*The Collected Letters of D.H. Lawrence*, ed. Harry T. Moore (2 vols., Heinemann, London, 1962)
Poems	*The Complete Poems of D.H. Lawrence*, ed. Vivian de Sola Pinto and Warren Roberts (2 vols., Heinemann, London, 1964)
Phoenix	*Phoenix: The Posthumous Papers of D.H. Lawrence*, ed. Edward D. McDonald (Heinemann, London, 1936)
Phoenix II	*Phoenix II: Uncollected, Unpublished and Other Prose Works by D.H. Lawrence*, ed. Warren Roberts and Harry T. Moore (Heinemann, London, 1968)

The majority of references to Lawrence's novels, tales and major non-fiction works are to the Penguin edition. In the case of *Sons and Lovers*, *The Rainbow* and *Women in Love*, the recently issued Penguin English Library texts have been preferred.

Cambridge University Press have started to issue a definitive scholarly edition of Lawrence's works. At the time of writing only a handful of titles have appeared, but I have used these where available. References to letters written before November 1916, and to *The Trespasser* and *The Lost Girl*, are therefore to the Cambridge edition.

'So intensely rapid is the change which is taking place in our environment and knowledge that in the course of a single life a man may pass through half a dozen stages of growth. Born and reared in possession of certain ideas and manners of action, he or she may, before middle life is reached, have had occasion repeatedly to modify, enlarge, and alter, or completely throw aside those traditions. Within the individuality itself of such persons, goes on, in an intensified form, that very struggle, conflict, and disco-ordination which is going on in society at large between its different members and sections . . . and the man or woman who attempts to adapt their life to the new material conditions and to harmony with the new knowledge, is almost bound at some time to rupture the continuity of their own psychological existence.

It is these conditions which give rise to the fact so often noticed, that the art of our age tends persistently to deal with subtle social problems, religious, political, and sexual, to which the art of the past holds no parallel.'

Olive Schreiner, *Woman and Labour* (1911)

INTRODUCTION

From the very first, Lawrence's work has been a focus for the discussion of sexual relationships and roles, and every serious reader and critic of Lawrence must, sooner or later, tackle the issue of 'Lawrence and women'. Attacks on Lawrence's misogyny and praise for his sensitive portrayals of femininity have co-existed since the inception of the critical debate.

The feminist case against Lawrence was first put at some length by John Middleton Murry in *Son of Woman* (1931). It is from Murry's account that the caricature of Lawrence as the squeaky-voiced, hysterical, impotent prophet of virility derives, and Murry who construed Lawrence's attitude towards women as a function of his precarious, 'hyper-sensitive masculinity'.[1]

> To annihilate the female insatiably demanding physical satisfaction from the man who cannot give it her — the female who has thus annihilated him — this is Lawrence's desire. To make her subject again, to re-establish his own manhood — this is the secret purpose of *Women in Love*. In imagination, he has his desire. He creates a sexual mystery beyond the phallic, wherein he is the lord; and he makes the woman acknowledge the existence of this ultra-phallic realm, and his own lordship in it.[2]

Murry's approach informs much subsequent feminist criticism of Lawrence, including the two classic accounts in Simone de Beauvoir's *The Second Sex* and Kate Millett's *Sexual Politics*.

Feminist appreciations of Lawrence, although much scarcer, have not been lacking. In the year following the appearance of Murry's *Son of Woman*, Anaïs Nin published *D.H. Lawrence: An Unprofessional Study*. According to Nin, Lawrence had 'a complete realization of the feelings of women. In fact, very often he wrote *as a woman* would write . . . It is the first time that a man has so wholly and completely expressed woman accurately.'[3] The tradition established by Nin is carried on by critics such as Lydia Blanchard, who writes: 'We need not agree with all of Lawrence's analysis . . . nor with all of his conclusions, to recognize the power in his descriptions of intelligent women trapped by a society that provides them inadequate outlets for their talents and energies.'[4] Such an approach, however, must now inevitably begin on the defensive:

> Those of us who admire the fiction of D.H. Lawrence, particularly those of us who are women, are faced with continuing difficulty in our attempts to separate his work from his reputation . . . Lawrence is the archetypal male chauvinist — that is doctrine now accepted by nearly every current book reviewer, popular critic, and cocktail party pundit, and even those women who admire the way in which Lawrence uses words are quick to add that they feel nothing but contempt for the way in which he uses women.[5]

Once the feminist cases for and against Lawrence have been stated, it does not take long for the debate to reach an impasse. Both approaches share two features which are characteristic of much Lawrence criticism. The first is the tendency for critics to take the text at its face value and to reproduce Lawrence's own terminology in their analyses, thereby making the corpus of Lawrence's work appear unnaturally self-contained and fuelling the myth of the man himself as an isolated and highly idiosyncratic writer. The second is the tendency to interpret his ideas (especially those about sexual relationships) in exclusively psychological or biographical terms, concentrating on his admittedly complicated relationships with his parents, his early lovers and his wife. Both methods have their merits, but between them they have brought about a state of near-stagnation in Lawrence criticism, in spite of the seemingly endless flow of academic and critical attention which his work continues to attract.

Feminist literary criticism as such is still finding its feet, but the documentation of women's history is well established, and can help to provide a fresh basis for literary analysis. Lawrence's literary career spanned one of the most crucial periods in that history. The years immediately preceding the First World War were characterised by intense feminist activity; the war itself was a watershed for women in virtually all aspects of life, precipitating change on an undreamt-of scale; the 1920s saw a consolidation of some of the freedoms that had been won, but also the beginnings of a fresh anti-feminist reaction. Lawrence's work was informed by these developments at every point, and whilst it would be naïve to see his writing as a simple response to them or reflection of them, it is perilous to ignore them. Most critics acknowledge that Lawrence is concerned with something called 'modern woman'; many make passing reference to 'the war' or 'the women's movement'. But those who rely on a psychological approach can get themselves into deep water trying to explain a change such as that which occurs in Lawrence's sexual theory between the *Study of Thomas Hardy* (written 1914) and *Fantasia of the Unconscious* (written 1921). H.M. Daleski, for example, after commenting that 'this discrepancy [between the Hardy study and *Fantasia*] is radical indeed, and has to be accounted for', suggests that 'it can best be explained in terms of a deep split in Lawrence himself'.

> I believe that Lawrence initially made a strenuous effort to reconcile the male and female elements in himself, but that he was more strongly feminine than masculine and that he was unable to effect such a reconciliation. I suggest, therefore, that his insistence in the *Fantasia* on an absolute degree of masculinity is evidence of an extreme reaction, a refusal even to acknowledge the existence of feminine components in his make-up.[6]

The two works in question are not even fictions. They are polemical pieces, and one of their principal determinants is the historical situation in which Lawrence found himself. ('What colossal idiocy, this war. Out of sheer rage I've begun my book about Thomas Hardy.')[7] Here, if anywhere, history is relevant. Yet Daleski makes no mention of the war, which divides the Hardy study from *Fantasia* and which also had a profound effect upon notions of masculinity and femininity. Even the most cursory reading in the literature of the period reveals that Lawrence's post-war paranoia was not merely personal, but shared with many men of his generation. It is not simply a case, in *Fantasia*, of Lawrence being unable to come to terms with the feminine components in his make-up; it is also, and perhaps more significantly, the articulation of a whole society's inability to come to terms with the massive change in sexual ideology which the war had engendered.

This book suggests a new basis for the discussion of Lawrence's work — in particular that part of it concerned with sexual relationships and roles — by examining it in relation to selected aspects of women's history and the development of feminism. It is therefore primarily an exercise in literary history, but also offers an analysis of Lawrence's work in the light of that history. I have concentrated on the novels and tales and the major essays on sexual theory, although the general outline would also, I believe, hold true for the poems, plays and other works.

Like many men of his generation, Lawrence, in the years before the

First World War, was intrigued and puzzled, rather than threatened, by feminism. While he appreciated the general aims of what was a very diverse movement, he was uncomfortable with the forms it took. The militant feminism of the suffragists seemed to him to lay too much stress on the outer political forms of equality, while the more romantic, spiritual side of the movement ignored the question of sexual liberation which preoccupied him. Nevertheless, for a brief period before and during the war — a period that was undoubtedly crucial in his development as a novelist — Lawrence espoused feminism, of a kind. At the end of 1912 he wrote from Italy to an old feminist friend in Eastwood: 'I shall do my work for women, better than the suffrage.'[8] This project was realised in the composition of the work that became *The Rainbow*, whose theme he summarised as 'woman becoming individual, self-responsible, taking her own initiative'.[9] During this period he urged men to 'draw nearer to women, expose themselves to them, and be altered by them'.[10] *The Rainbow* and *Women in Love* have been so extensively discussed elsewhere that I have confined myself here to dealing with particular points of special interest that arise from them. *The Rainbow* is unique among Lawrence's major fictions in its presentation of the historical process — a process which stretches by way of an essentially matrilineal descent from the first Brangwen woman who turns to 'the spoken world beyond', through to Ursula's complex, isolated and essentially modern struggle for self-definition. It is this sense of history and women's place in it, as much as Lawrence's forging of an essentially new form of language for the novel, which marks off *The Rainbow* from the many other fictional studies of 'woman taking her own initiative' which were appearing at this time.

If the feminist movement in the most general sense of the term is an important influence for *The Rainbow*, the war is clearly crucial to *Women in Love*. Amongst the titles which Lawrence considered for the novel were *Love Among the Ruins*, *The Latter Days* and *Dies Irae*, and the sense of an era — or rather of a whole civilisation — coming to an end, permeates the book. In 1916 Lawrence could only conjecture the nature of the phoenix — if any — which would rise from the ashes, and as a result the novel attains a supreme poise. Originating in a peculiarly creative tension between despair and hope, it combines nostalgia for the past with a deeply-felt concern about how the future might be lived.

A new world did emerge from the war, but it was not the world that Lawrence had hoped for. Almost overnight, large numbers of the women on whom he had pinned much of his faith in the future found themselves in the labour force, doing new jobs at men's rates of pay, with new expectations, including a new sense of sexual freedom. The second part of this study therefore concerns itself with the war, both as a massive instigator of social change which was responsible for far-reaching upheavals in the position of women, and as a point of no return in the evolution of Lawrence's work. Women had entered 'the man's world' with a vengeance, and Lawrence's writing betrays his unease at this development.

The change which the war brought about in Lawrence's ideas can be most dramatically illustrated by comparing his pre- and post-war theoretical writing on sexuality. In 1914 he still has strong affinities with the progressive, liberal, pro-feminist sex-psychologists such as Edward Carpenter and Havelock Ellis, who, while for the most part accepting traditional definitions of masculinity and femininity, argued in favour of equality between the sexes and for the 'feminisation' of patriarchal society. In his later work, however, Lawrence adopts completely new definitions of 'masculinity' and 'femininity' and proposes a rigid and deterministic sexual hierarchy.

By the 1920s, Lawrence had become convinced that a feminist revolution had actually occurred, and had gone badly wrong. He believed that the dominant ideology of the post-war world was feminine — not, however, a true femininity of instinct and feeling, but a perverted femininity of will and idealism — and that a masculine renaissance was necessary to restore the balance. This belief was shared by other writers, and appears to be part of a general upsurge in male insecurity at the time. I examine the historical evidence for Lawrence's assertion that women had become the dominant sex, and discuss his various programmes for masculinist revolution. I also discuss the similarities between his late writings and the sensationalist romances of the twenties such as *The Sheik*, his espousal of the 'phallic consciousness' and his development of the phallus as a symbol adequate to represent the full complexity of the new masculinity.

I have, throughout, found comparisons with popular literature to be fruitful. Technically, and in his degree of outspokenness on sexual matters, Lawrence was an *avant-garde* writer. But in general terms his themes and preoccupations are quite often those of the popular novelists, and the view of him, particularly in the post-war years, as an angry voice crying in the wilderness, needs, I think, to be modified. Although the question of Lawrence's historical relationship with women's literature is not an issue which I have pursued here, I have included a discussion of the way in which Lawrence used women as actual or potential collaborators, and their writing as source material. This seems to me to be a phenomenon which would repay further study by feminist critics, since it lays bare in a particularly graphic way assumptions about femininity as the 'raw material' of art and masculinity as its 'shaping force'.

Notes

1. John Middleton Murry, *Son of Woman* (Jonathan Cape, London, 1931), p. 72.
2. Ibid., p. 118.
3. Anaïs Nin, *D.H. Lawrence: An Unprofessional Study* (Edward W. Titus, Paris, 1932), pp. 66–7 and 70.
4. Lydia Blanchard, 'Love and Power: A Reconsideration of Sexual Politics in D.H. Lawrence', *Modern Fiction Studies*, vol. 21, no. 3 (1975), p. 443.
5. Ibid., p. 431.
6. H.M. Daleski, *The Forked Flame* (Faber and Faber, London, 1965), p. 33.
7. Letter to J.B. Pinker, 5 September 1914. *Letters*, vol. 2, p. 212.
8. Letter to Sallie Hopkin, 23 December 1912. *Letters*, vol. 1, p. 490.
9. Letter to Edward Garnett, 22 April 1914. *Letters*, vol. 2, p. 165.
10. Letter to Arthur McLeod, 2 June 1914. Ibid., p. 181.

1 THE SUFFRAGIST

The women's suffrage movement reached its culmination in the militant campaign of the Women's Social and Political Union (WSPU) during the period from its foundation in 1903 to the outbreak of war in 1914. The history of the movement has been well documented, and will not be summarised here. But these were the years of Lawrence's youth and the composition of his first novels, and the extent to which the suffrage movement impinged on his early life is worth noting.

There was a strong branch of the WSPU in Nottingham, and leaders of the campaign, including Mrs Pankhurst herself, spoke regularly there. Eastwood had its own branch, and in October 1909 *Votes for Women*, the official WSPU newspaper, reported 'a most successful meeting at Eastwood — the first visit of a Hunger-striker'.[1] When Lawrence moved to Croydon he would have found an equally active branch of the organisation with offices in the town centre and a full-time paid secretary; at Croydon there was also a group for women teachers and a branch of the Men's League for Woman Suffrage. Other bodies besides the WSPU were active in the field of women's rights; there was a branch of the National Union of Women's Suffrage Societies, a more conservative and constitutional organisation, in Nottingham, which numbered Alice Dax among its members, and Lawrence's mother was an official of the local Co-operative Women's Guild, a detail which finds its way into *Sons and Lovers*. The Guild's aim was to bring about a 'peaceful revolution from autocratic Capitalism to democratic Co-operation',[2] and it sought to unite women through their common interests as consumers; it also campaigned for the setting up of local health facilities and for maternity benefits.

Lawrence's friends and acquaintances in Nottingham included people of all degrees of political commitment. He was a close friend of the Hopkins and the Daxes, who formed the nucleus of a small progressive socialist group in Eastwood. Sallie Hopkin's daughter Enid Hilton has left an account of the involvement of her mother and Alice Dax in the feminist movement. According to her they were '*years* ahead of their time . . . widely read, "advanced" in dress, thought and house decoration. Alice was almost completely uninhibited in an age when you just weren't . . . clear, direct, uncluttered in thought and action, to the point of harshness.'[3] Enid Hilton claims that Lawrence must have met many of the prominent figures of the suffrage campaign, such as Mrs Despard and Annie Kenney, and also mentions Philip Snowden, Ramsay MacDonald, Beatrice and Sidney Webb, the Pankhursts, Keir Hardie, Edward Carpenter and Margaret Bondfield as guests of the Hopkins'. She remembers being taken to Nottingham for large suffrage meetings but also talks of groups 'in our small town', that is Eastwood, where there was 'much enthusiasm, many fights and some really productive effort'.[4] However, the main companions of Lawrence's youth were not active feminists. Jessie Chambers, for example, was what might be called an 'advanced' young woman, but her interests were literary and philosophical rather than political. It is significant that Helen Corke's account of Jessie's politics tails off into her interest in Russian literature:

> Jessie Chambers was very conscious of the social injustice done to the labouring classes, and particularly to miners in local areas. Her sympathies were with the Labour Party, and she followed closely the course of industrial politics, but she took no active part either in reform movements or local politics. In this country one might fairly call her a Socialist . . . She admired the Russian classic literature. Turgenev and Dostoievsky, to which Lawrence had introduced her; through these authors she formed her conception of the Russian people.[5]

In *D.H. Lawrence: A Personal Record* Jessie candidly admits her political naïvety as a young woman when she describes her meeting with Ford Madox Hueffer and Violet Hunt, who were at that time involved in the suffrage campaign.

> Here Hueffer unpinned a paper and showed me an announcement of a Suffragette meeting.
> 'I suppose you're interested in that,' he said.
> 'Oh, yes, I've a very enthusiastic friend who tells me all about it,' I replied. Then a little later he said:
> 'You're a sort of Socialist, I suppose?'
> Not a single political idea had crossed my mind in those days; but I liked the pleasant ambiguity of his definition and decided there and then that it described me exactly.[6]

It seems as if Alice Dax tried to make both Jessie and Lawrence more politically aware by introducing them to the *New Age* in 1908 or 1909.

Jessie says that Lawrence, however, 'liked it far more for its literature than its politics. He was never really interested in politics, and was quickly irritated and bored by the subject.'[7] Nevertheless, J.D. Chambers, her brother, remembers 'rampageous arguments on politics, especially votes for women, with Lawrence leading the younger generation against their parents'.[8]

Helen Corke, another of Lawrence's women friends at this time, regarded even Jessie's degree of political awareness with awe. She was also an advanced and emancipated woman, but distrusted collective action and disapproved of the tactics of the suffragettes.

> The actions of the Suffragettes are shouted from the house-tops, but I am not moved by the gospel according to Mrs Pankhurst and her daughters. It is an injustice that women may not vote, but I cannot feel that the vote is worth the price paid for it by these women. Into the flame of their enthusiasm for 'the cause' the Suffragettes fling individual dignity, beauty, reserve and poise — attributes that no woman should sacrifice.[9]

Louie Burrows, to whom Lawrence was engaged from 1909 to 1912, was more involved. Lawrence sent her a long account of the Croydon by-election of 29 March 1909, in which the Conservative candidate had declared his opposition to women's suffrage. His letter describes how he got caught up in the crowd at the hustings, and paints a rather romantic picture of the suffrage campaigners:

> I was in the mad grip of the crowd before the Suffragettes. If you had felt the surge, the vicious rush of one solid mass of men towards the car where the two women were alone, one standing crying scorn on the brutes, the other sitting with dark, sad eyes![10]

In a letter of 14 June 1911 Lawrence asks Louie, 'Oh, by the way, would you like to come down to the Suffragette procession on Saturday? I enclose bills. It will, I think, be very nice.'[11] He also sent her a copy of Olive Schreiner's *Woman and Labour*, one of the seminal feminist texts of the period, and discussed it with her in letters at her request. Louie retained an active interest in feminism in later life and campaigned for the rights of women teachers.[12]

In his early life Lawrence was therefore surrounded by women who were involved in the suffrage campaign to various degrees, in what must have been a typical spectrum of interest ranging from the deep commitment of Sallie Hopkin and Alice Dax to the more marginal interest of Jessie Chambers and Louie Burrows. The general issue of women's rights was very much in the public eye, and the suffrage movement featured in much of the fiction of the period. There were two principal stereotypes of the suffragette: the well-meaning but ridiculous enthusiast, like Miss Miniver in H.G. Wells's *Ann Veronica* (1909), too blinkered to perceive that life contains more important things than the Vote, and the morbid man-hater, like Olive Chancellor in Henry James's *The Bostonians* (1886), whose personal neuroses lead her to seek vengeance on men. The suffrage movement is often used as a foil to the more individual forms of liberation examined by the novelist. The sentiments expressed by the heroine of Grant Allen's ironical anti-feminist novel *The Woman Who Did* (1895) are typical.

> It's the question of social and moral emancipation that interests me far more than the mere political one — woman's rights as they call it . . . After all, political life fills but a small and unimportant part in our total existence. It's the perpetual pressure of social and ethical restrictions that most weighs down women.[13]

A similar conclusion is reached by Ann Veronica. Her brief involvement with the suffrage campaign results in a spell in prison, during which she realises: 'I like men. I can talk with them. I've never found them hostile. I've got no feminine class feeling . . . A woman wants a proper alliance with a man, a man who is better stuff than herself.'[14] Her reaction to the suffrage movement from that moment on is the same as Ursula's in *The Rainbow*; an acknowledgement of its importance tempered by the conviction that she personally transcends it:

> She was . . . stirred by the idea of the equal citizenship of men and women, by the realisation that a big and growing organisation of women were giving form and a generalised expression to just that personal pride, that aspiration for personal freedom and respect which had brought her to London; but when she heard Miss Miniver discoursing on the next step in the suffrage campaign, or read of women badgering Cabinet Ministers, padlocked to railings, or getting up in a public meeting to pipe out a demand for votes and be carried out kicking and screaming, her soul revolted. She could not part with dignity. Something as yet unformulated within her kept her estranged from all these practical aspects of her beliefs . . . It was as

if she faced a darkness in which was something very beautiful and wonderful as yet unimagined.[15]

Such attitudes may be partly attributed to the form of the novel itself, its emergence as an expression of bourgeois individualism and its concern with the conflict between the individual and society rather than with conflicting classes or groups within society. Individual liberation of this kind is also less threatening; it has been said that 'an individual "emancipated" woman is an amusing incongruity, a titillating commodity, easily consumed'.[16] Nevertheless, it is interesting to note that similar views found expression within the broad church of feminism itself. The *Freewoman*, later the *New Freewoman*,[17] set itself up as the mouthpiece of those women who were not interested in mass movements and who attributed oppression to individual weakness rather than to social causes. An editorial in 1913 set out the journal's philosophy:

> There is only one person concerned in the freeing of individuals: and that is the person who wears and feels and resents the shackles. Shackles must be burst off: if they are cut away from outside, they will immediately reform . . . 'Causes' are the diversion of the feeble — of those who have lost the power of acting from their own nature. They are for the titillation of the senses of the herd, and a person who can act strongly should shun all Cause-ites and their works . . . Accurately speaking, there *is* no 'Woman Movement'. 'Woman' is doing nothing — she has, indeed, no existence. A very limited number of individual women are emphasising the fact that the first thing to be taken into account with regard to them is that they *are* individuals and can not be lumped together into a class, a sex, or a 'movement'.[18]

There are marked similarities between the general tone of the *New Freewoman* and the trend of Lawrence's thought. The magazine is anti-idealistic and anti-intellectual: 'Our business is to annihilate thought . . . to dissolve ideas . . . Men need no ideas . . . what men need is power of Being, strength in themselves.'[19] It condemns democracy: 'For the sake of meddling in the affairs of others, each one abandons power over himself.'[20] It sees women's new awakening as spiritual rather than social or political, and materialism as the greatest enemy to individual emancipation. It even contained advertisements from people wishing to purchase islands or land where they could set up utopias which resemble Lawrence's Rananim. Many of its contributors were indeed friends of Lawrence or moved in the same circles: they included Barbara Low, Edward Carpenter, Ezra Pound, Ford Madox Hueffer, Richard Aldington (who became assistant editor) and Violet Hunt. Reviews of Lawrence's work appeared in the magazine;[21] indeed, the artistic side began to predominate, and it became to some extent a vehicle for imagism, with frequent contributions by Amy Lowell, Hilda Doolittle and Pound himself, as well as pieces by Rebecca West and Remy de Gourmont. It carried articles on Marinetti and the Futurists and extracts from Bergson, and to some extent set itself up as an apolitical *New Age*. At the end of 1913 it dropped its claim to being an exclusively feminist periodical — 'the present title of the paper causes it to be confounded with organs devoted solely to the advocacy of an unimportant reform in an obsolete political institution'[22] — and changed its title to the *Egoist*. Under this title it ran from 1914 to the end of 1919, T.S. Eliot succeeding Richard Aldington as assistant editor in 1917. Joyce's *Portrait of the Artist as a Young Man* was published serially in the magazine in 1914-15.

Lawrence's views on the suffragist movement are most clearly set out in the *Study of Thomas Hardy*. He admires the crusading spirit of the suffragists — 'certainly the bravest, and, in the old sense, most heroic party amongst us' — and sees their aims as 'worthy and admirable'.[23] But for Lawrence they are only measures to patch up a social system which is already rotten at the core. He is committed to complete social and spiritual revolution, not piecemeal reform. 'Law can only modify the conditions, for better or worse, of that which already exists.'[24] And for Lawrence the revolution must start with the individual. He locates the sickness of the twentieth century 'in the heart of man, and not in the conditions'.[25]

> Is there any great sickness in the body politic? Then where and what is it? Am I, or your suffragist woman, or your voting man, sex-whole and money-healthy, are we sound human beings? Have we achieved to true individuality and to a sufficient completeness in ourselves? Because, if not — then, physician, heal thyself.[26]

The language and imagery are traditional, almost identical to Matthew Arnold's in *Culture and Anarchy*, the opposition between the organic and the mechanical being central to Lawrence's argument. Law is a 'very, very clumsy and mechanical instrument' which cannot 'empower the poppy to flower'.[27] The poppy is Lawrence's chosen symbol throughout the Hardy study for the full achievement of individuality and wholeness, bursting into a flame-coloured flower that serves no utilitarian purpose, but somehow connects us with the unknown, 'the colour and shine of being'.[28] Lawrence declares that, if the women's movement aligned itself with spiritual revolution rather than with mechanical reform, 'I should be glad, and the opposition would be vital and intense, instead of just flippantly or exasperatedly static'. Then 'the woman's movement would be a living human movement'.[29] This position towards the suffrage movement was a common one. Wyndham Lewis's *Blast*, for example, praised the suffragists' energy — 'You and artists are the only things (you don't mind being called things?) left in England with a little life in them'[30] — but it too questioned the goal of legal reform that the suffrage movement set itself. It was also a view shared by many women. The *Freewoman*'s contributors and readers would have sympathised with Lawrence's stance.

In Lawrence's early work there are several characters, some major, others minor, who consciously identify themselves or are identified by others as feminists. (Their actual connection to one of the suffrage organisations may be tenuous or even non-existent, but because of the contemporary predominance of the suffragists they tend to be associated with them.) But the issues raised by feminism are reduced to personal problems to which individual answers must be sought. *The White Peacock* stresses the inability of the individual to do anything about social injustice or misery. When, towards the end of the novel, George taxes Lettie with 'the monstrous denial of life to the many by the fortunate few', she replies: 'Of course . . . I have read Mr Wells and Mr Shaw . . . But what can I do? I think the rich have as much misery as the poor, and of quite as deadly a sort. What can I do?'[31] George persuades Lettie into a brief flirtation with socialism and feminism but she confesses to her brother Cyril that 'at the bottom, you know, . . . I don't care for anything very much except myself'.

> I have had such a lark. Two or three times I have been to the Hollies; to socialist meetings. Leslie does not know. They are great fun. Of course, I am in sympathy with the socialists, but I cannot narrow my eyes till I see one thing only. Life is like a large, rather beautiful man who is young and full of vigour, but hairy, barbaric, with hands hard and dirty, the dirt ingrained. I know his hands are very ugly, I know his mouth is not firmly shapen, I know his limbs are hairy and brutal: but his eyes are deep and very beautiful. That is what I tell George.[32]

Lettie makes the usual objections to the people involved in the socialist and feminist movements; they are comic, narrow-minded, over-earnest and cannot see life whole.

> The people are so earnest, they make me sad. But then, they are so didactic, they hold forth so much, they are so cock-sure and so narrow-eyed, they make me laugh. George laughs too. I am sure we made such fun of a straight-haired goggle of a girl who had suffered in prison for the cause of women, that I am ashamed when I see my 'Women's League' badge.[33]

Socialism and feminism remain abstract notions in *The White Peacock* because the situations which might show why they are necessary are missing from the novel. The brief tour of the London slums in Part 3 which is supposed to inspire George's socialism is hardly convincing; Lettie's discontent is shown to have something to do with her role as a woman, her lack of any real occupation, her choice of husband and her self-abnegation in marriage and motherhood, but this is left vague. The only strategy for coping with these discontents that is implied in the novel is Emily's escapist return, through her marriage to a solid farmer, to the simple life.

> Emily had at last found her place, and had escaped from the torture of strange, complex modern life. She was making a pie, and the flour was white on her brown arms. She pushed the tickling hair from her face with her arm, and looked at me with tranquil pleasure, as she worked the paste in the yellow bowl.[34]

In the portrayal of Mrs Morel and Clara in *Sons and Lovers*, on the other hand, many of the material conditions of women's oppression which inspired the women's movement are revealed. The close attention to detail and the faithful rendering of the texture of everyday existence give us a vividly accurate picture of working-class life. But the predominant note is still the personal one. Miriam's reflection on land nationalisation is typical of the novel's emphasis on individualism: 'After all . . . if the land were nationalized, Edgar and Paul and I would be just the same.'[35] Organisations which exist to promote social change come to be seen as irrelevant; it is suggested that the problems with which they are concerned can be solved on a personal level.

Feminism first enters *Sons and Lovers* in the form of the Women's

Guild to which Mrs Morel belongs. The details are those of Mrs Lawrence's own life.

> When the children were old enough to be left, Mrs Morel joined the Women's Guild. It was a little club of women attached to the Co-operative Wholesale Society, which met on Monday night in the long room over the grocery shop of the Bestwood 'Co-op'. The women were supposed to discuss the benefits to be derived from co-operation, and other social questions. Sometimes Mrs Morel read a paper.[36]

Mrs Morel enjoys these meetings; they give her an opportunity to use her intelligence and her sharp tongue in discussion, and she gains a new stature in the eyes of her children: 'It seemed queer to the children to see their mother, who was always busy about the house, sitting writing in her rapid fashion, thinking, referring to books, and writing again. They felt for her on such occasions the deepest respect.'[37] The Guild is, however, resented by many of the men.

> The Guild was called by some hostile husbands, who found their wives getting too independent, the 'clat-fart' shop — that is, the gossip-shop. It is true, from off the basis of the Guild, the women could look at their homes, at the conditions of their own lives, and find fault. So the colliers found their women had a new standard of their own, rather disconcerting.[38]

The Guild no doubt served a useful purpose in raising the political awareness of ordinary women. But the whole of the first part of *Sons and Lovers* proclaims that to the problem of Mrs Morel's life the Co-operative Women's Guild can at best be only a very superficial answer; as John Goode says, 'She has her own ways out — significantly through the moral vitality of the chapel and the feminist emancipation of the Women's Guild, but these are only consolatory.'[39] The novel itself, however, portrays with unusual clarity the economic basis of women's oppression. In Chapter One, pregnant with her third child, Mrs Morel reflects that 'she could not afford to have this third. She did not want it.'[40] The first quarrel between the Morels centres on Mr Morel's financial deceit; he has not paid for the furniture, and rents the house in which they live rather than owning it as Mrs Morel has been led to believe. Mrs Morel is constantly at a disadvantage because of her lack of financial independence. Logically, she cannot even upbraid her husband for stealing money from her purse when she is totally dependent on him to give her that money in the first place. In their battles Morel exploits this position as breadwinner and Mrs Morel's essential powerlessness is revealed.

> 'The house is filthy with you,' she cried.
> 'Then get out on it — it's mine. Get out on it!' he shouted. 'It's me as brings th' money whoam, not thee. It's my house, not thine. Then ger out on't — ger out on't!'
> 'And I would,' she cried, suddenly shaken into tears of impotence. 'Ah, wouldn't I, wouldn't I have gone long ago, but for those children.'[41]

But despite her poverty, Mrs Morel will not stoop to being exploited by the out-work which the other women of her area undertake: 'I'd starve before I'd sit down and seam twenty-four stockings for twopence ha'-penny.'[42]

There is little that Mrs Morel can do to change the fundamental condition of her life. With Clara the position is different. Being childless, she has been able to leave her husband and work for her living, and feminism has given her the support she needs to do this. At first it seems as if the fact of Clara's feminism is going to be of some importance in the novel. In the end it is not — but its fate is interesting. Clearly, some important areas of Clara's character, including her feminism, are based on Alice Dax, who recognised herself in the character.[43] For example, Clara's indifference to Paul's art reflects the lack of support for his writing that Lawrence sensed in Mrs Dax, who was in favour of strict naturalism. 'How can a woman whose feelings flow in such straight canals follow me in my threadings, my meanderings, my spurts and my sleepings!' he complained.[44] On the other hand, Clara's blonde statuesque beauty seems to be inspired by Frieda, and Jessie Chambers asserted that at least one incident in the novel, the visit of Paul and Clara to the theatre, was based on an outing that Lawrence and Frieda made to see Shaw's *Man and Superman* in Nottingham.[45] But this episode could just as easily have been based on a visit that he and Alice Dax made to see *Electra* at Covent Garden, after which he wrote to Jessie saying that he had 'very nearly' been unfaithful to her.[46]

Clara has left her husband because of his cruelty and unfaithfulness. She is an 'advanced woman', a suffragette who 'talks on platforms', having been in the women's movement before her marriage and remained active in it for ten years. Through her, Paul gets 'into connexion with the Socialist, Suffragette, Unitarian people in Nottingham'.[47] But Clara is an individualist too, and her feminism has led her, not to identify with other women, but to separate herself from them — 'she considered herself as a woman apart, and particularly apart, from her class'[48] — a stance based to some extent on the education she has been able to obtain through the women's movement. Her feminism begins by intriguing Paul, but later it comes to seem an irrelevance, and towards the end of the novel we hear less about it. Eventually the novel implies that Clara's dissatisfaction has nothing to do with women's oppression, but concerns only her own sexuality and the necessity for her to come to terms with it; she has only to 'sort herself out', not to try to change society. Her affair with Paul is a kind of therapy, enabling her finally to return to her husband. Because the novel betrays little appreciation of the relationship between the personal and the political, the character of Clara lacks coherence; her feminism, one of the major characteristics through which she is first defined for us, ultimately has no real function. Kate Millett has remarked on the shifting centre of Clara's character:

> Clara . . . is really two people, the rebellious feminist and political activist whom Paul accuses of penis envy and even man-hating, and who tempts him the more for being a harder conquest, and, at a later stage, the sensuous rose, who by the end of the novel is changed once again — now beyond recognition — into a 'loose woman' whom Paul nonchalantly disposes of when he has exhausted her sexual utility.[49]

The contradictory attitudes towards Clara can be examined in more detail. When Paul first meets Clara she is out walking with Miriam, and he is struck by her confident assertiveness, which contrasts strongly with Miriam's shrinking manner. Clara is a 'striking woman', the way she holds herself is 'defiant', she is tall, with 'handsome shoulders', and (most provocative of all) she is not in the least interested in Paul. Miriam notices the response to this apparent challenge: 'The girl saw his masculine spirit rear its head.'[50] As Clara remains indifferent to Paul, his perception of her becomes more complex. We get a closer picture of her, moving in to her face. Her grey eyes are still only 'scornful', but Paul becomes conscious of her sensual appeal — 'a skin like white honey' — and then, in observing her mouth, uses the sensuality to cast doubt upon the integrity of the scornfulness, implying that Clara is out of touch with her body and its needs: 'a full mouth, with a slightly lifted upper lip that did not know whether it was raised in scorn of all men or out of eagerness to be kissed, but which believed the former'.[51] Paul obviously believes the latter, and the implication that Clara should be concerned with her own unacknowledged sexuality rather than with a spurious feminism is already present. We are then distanced from Clara again: we are told that she is dressed in simple clothes, the sort of thing, one imagines, that Alice Dax used to wear, inspired by the Dress Reform movement; but these are not to Paul's taste, and again he casts doubts upon Clara's motives in choosing them, suggesting that it is an affectation: 'a sort of slightly affected simple dress that made her look rather sack-like'.[52] Paul then dismisses her economic status and her aesthetic sense — 'she was evidently poor, and had not much taste' — reminding himself that 'Miriam usually looked nice'.[53]

It is only when Paul has parted from the two women that he remembers that 'Mrs Dawes was separated from her husband, and had taken up Women's Rights. She was supposed to be clever.'[54] This interests Paul, and the next time he and Miriam meet they discuss Clara. Miriam sympathises with her feminism and thinks her a 'fine woman', but Paul refuses to call her 'fine' except in so far as her physical traits are concerned. He praises the 'fight' and aggressiveness he sees in her face, her 'fierceness', 'her skin and the texture of her'. 'Look at her mouth — made for passion — and the very set-back of her throat.'[55] For Paul, Clara's assertiveness and her physical presence are an indication of *sexual* energy.

After a quarrel, Miriam invites Paul to meet Clara at Willey Farm. Miriam has already concluded that Paul's interest in Clara is physical, and has arranged a test (a parallel to his 'Test on Miriam') to see whether he will succumb to what she views as the temptation offered by the older woman. This time Paul starts by meeting Clara on her own ground: 'You were at Margaret Bonford's meeting the other evening.'[56] The discussion about Margaret Bonford — who is obviously Margaret Bondfield, at that time president of the Adult Suffrage League[57] — is a good example of the way in which Paul consistently ignores the larger implications of feminism and reduces it to a series of personal issues.

> 'I think she's a lovable little woman,' said Paul.
> 'Margaret Bonford!' exclaimed Clara. 'She's a great deal cleverer than most men.'
> 'Well, I didn't say she wasn't,' he said, deprecating. 'She's lovable for all that.'
> 'And, of course, that is all that matters,' said Clara witheringly.[58]

Paul and Clara are talking about different women. Clara is talking about Margaret Bonford the public figure, while Paul can only see Margaret Bonford the character, the individual, the human phenomenon, divorced from any political or social context. Both points of view are equally limited, and while it has been argued that Clara's is a 'rigid, egocentric isolation which has cut her off from all warm contact with others, leaving her with minimal verbal, intellectual, political, and commercial relationships only,'[59] Paul's individualism and emphasis on 'character' tend to blind him to any larger relationships than the personal. He cannot see why Clara speaks 'as if he were responsible for some deprivation which Miss Bonford suffered',[60] because of his failure to grasp that he exists not only as an individual but also as a member of various social groups and classes.

> 'Well,' he said, 'I thought she was warm, and awfully nice – only too frail. I wished she was sitting comfortably in peace –'
> ' "Darning her husband's stockings," ' said Clara scathingly.
> 'I'm sure she wouldn't mind darning even my stockings,' he said. 'And I'm sure she'd do them well. Just as I wouldn't mind blacking her boots if she wanted me to.'[61]

Paul thus reduces the larger issue of women's rights to the level of domestic give-and-take (he obviously has in mind his relationship with his mother). Clara will not answer him and he, offended, escapes to meet Edgar, with whom he debates the question of whether Clara is really a man-hater.

Later Mrs Leivers makes some allusions to Clara's personal life and her separation from her husband. Paul, although he characteristically chooses to be left with the women instead of going out with the men, deflates the intimate, serious mood of their conversation.

> After tea, when all the men had gone but Paul, Mrs Leivers said to Clara:
> 'And you find life happier now?'
> 'Infinitely.'
> 'And you are satisfied?'
> 'So long as I can be free and independent.'
> 'And you don't *miss* anything in your life?' asked Mrs Leivers gently.
> 'I've put all that behind me.'
> Paul had been feeling uncomfortable during this discourse. He

got up.

'You'll find you're always tumbling over things you've put behind you,' he said. Then he took his departure to the cowsheds. He felt he had been witty, and his manly pride was high. He whistled as he went down the brick track.[62]

One of the principal ways in which Paul avoids the issues raised by feminism is by appealing to the principle of chivalry. He has already shown a tendency to cope with the world of the factory by romanticising it:

> Connie, with her mane of red hair, her face of apple-blossom, her murmuring voice, such a lady in her shabby black frock, appealed to his romantic side.
> 'When you sit winding,' he said, 'it looks as if you were spinning at a spinning-wheel — it looks ever so nice. You remind me of Elaine in the "Idylls of the King".'[63]

Knowing that one reminds the office boy of a medieval heroine does not necessarily make factory work any more pleasant, and when, later, Paul sees Clara, now back at Jordan's, as a Penelope at her loom, she is impatient. 'Would it make any difference?' she retorts.[64]

Paul explicitly sets up this chivalric attitude in opposition to Clara's feminism. On the day of Clara's visit to Willey Farm, when he and Clara and Miriam are out walking, he remarks:

> 'What a treat to be a knight . . . and to have a pavilion here.'
> 'And to have us shut up safely?' replied Clara.
> 'Yes,' he answered, 'singing with your maids at your broidery. I would carry your banner of white and green and heliotrope. I would have "W.S.P.U." emblazoned on my shield, beneath a woman rampant.'
> 'I have no doubt,' said Clara, 'that you would much rather fight for a woman than let her fight for herself.'
> 'I would. When she fights for herself she seems like a dog before a looking-glass, gone into a mad fury with its own shadow.'
> 'And *you* are the looking-glass?' she asked, with a curl of the lip.
> 'Or the shadow,' he replied.[65]

The tone here is light and jocular, but two different concepts are discernible. Paul suggests that in setting themselves up against men, women gain nothing, since the lots of the two sexes are bound up with each other — man is woman's own 'shadow'. Clara takes his reference to the mirror differently, suggesting that what he really means is that man is the mirror in which woman must seek her true self.

It is when Clara reveals emotion or weakness that Paul starts to feel attracted towards her and not merely interested. After the above exchange, he looks at her and sees that 'the upward lifting of her face was misery and not scorn' and 'his heart grew tender'.[66] Paul's reaction is not unlike that of Everard Barfoot in *The Odd Women* or Basil Ransome in *The Bostonians*. It is one of the stock responses to an emancipated woman — a desire to experience the thrill of seeing a strong and independent person betray her vulnerability. When Paul visits Clara's home and sees her jennying lace, he reflects that 'she seemed denied and deprived of so much. And her arm moved mechanically, that should never have been subdued to a mechanism, and her head was bowed to the lace, that never should have been bowed.'[67] When Paul asks her about her work — 'Is it sweated?' — Clara tries to make a general point: 'More or less. Isn't *all* women's work? That's another trick the men have played, since we force ourselves into the labour market.'[68] But Paul sees it as an individual problem that he can solve by getting Clara back to Jordan's. When Clara's mother reveals that Clara would in fact like to return to the factory but is too proud to ask, Paul experiences 'a thrill of joy, thinking that she might need his help';[69] and when she is back at work he asserts his rights as her supervisor in order to break down her aloofness and reserve.

Not only does Paul want to see Clara betray her vulnerability; he also wants her to acknowledge that her feminism is misguided and that what she really needs is sexual fulfilment. When Paul, Miriam and Clara, still on their walk, encounter Miss Limb and her horse, Paul gets the hint for which he has been waiting. The three discuss Miss Limb's eccentricity and her obsessive attachment to her stallion. Clara suddenly says, 'I suppose . . . she wants a man', which silences the other two.[70] This comment amounts to an admission from Clara that she is aware of the consequences of sexual deprivation, and it arouses Paul's excitement. Later, speaking about Clara to Miriam, he uses the same phrase that the three of them had previously used about Miss Limb — 'something's the matter with her'[71] — implying that the answer in Clara's case is the same: she too wants a man. From this point onwards Clara's aggressive feminism, which had previously intrigued Paul, is less important. In his eyes it comes increasingly to signify that she is not bound by traditional sexual morality. When Mrs Morel asks 'Won't people talk?' about his liaison with Clara, he says: 'They know she's a suffragette, and so on . . . she lives separate from her husband, and talks on platforms; so she's already singled out from the sheep, and, as far as I can see, hasn't much to lose.'[72]

Much has been written about Paul's 'baptism of fire in passion' with Clara and the relative success or failure of this relationship and the relationship with Miriam. In fact the relationships are similar in many crucial respects and both can be said to 'fail' for essentially the same reasons. Paul conceives of sexual desire as something impersonal: 'a sort of detached thing, that did not belong to a woman';[73] 'the great hunger and impersonality of passion'.[74] With Miriam, who is reluctant and apprehensive about their love-making, 'he had always, almost wilfully, to put her out of count, and act from the brute strength of his own feelings'.[75] Paul resents the fact that Miriam insists on calling him back to 'the littleness, the personal relationship'.[76] Clara is more sexually experienced, and not afraid of physical passion in the way that Miriam is; and for a brief spell it seems as if she and Paul experience what he calls 'the something big and intense that changes you when you really come together with somebody else'.[77] This crucial epiphany is usually located in the scene of their love-making by the canal, when the following famous passage occurs.

> He lifted his head, and looked into her eyes. They were dark and shining and strange, life wild at the source staring into his life, stranger to him, yet meeting him; and he put his face down on her throat, afraid. What was she? A strong, strange, wild life, that breathed with his in the darkness through this hour. It was all so much bigger than themselves that he was hushed. They had met, and included in their meeting the thrust of the manifold grass-stems, the cry of the peewit, the wheel of the stars.[78]

Lawrence writes: 'It was for *each of them* an initiation and a satisfaction . . . There was a verification which they had had *together*.'[79] But the text itself gives the lie to this, for the satisfaction is Paul's; the impersonal satisfaction of an impersonal urge, the only difference being that Clara has not resisted in the way that Miriam did.

> But then Clara was not there for him, only a woman, warm, something he loved and almost worshipped, there in the dark. But it was not Clara, and she submitted to him . . . she took him simply because his need was bigger either than her or him, and her soul was still within her.[80]

On the very next page it is admitted that 'Clara was not satisfied'.[81] From this point on Paul begins to feel more and more that 'his experience had been impersonal, and not Clara', while she feels the need for a more personal intimacy, needs to feel surer of Paul the individual – 'he might leave her'.[82] The relationship in effect reaches the same impasse that the relationship with Miriam had reached. Paul complains, 'Love should give a sense of freedom, not of prison. Miriam made me feel tied up like a donkey to a stake. I must feed on her patch, and nowhere else. It's sickening.' To Clara's retort, 'And would *you* let a *woman* do as she likes?', Paul says 'Yes'.[83] He is genuinely unconcerned about the double standard of morality. He does not expect his women to be 'pure'. In fact, Paul's concept of sexual love, which originates as a way of coping with his own psycho-sexual problems but ends up as a *desideratum*, really *requires* that both partners should be equal, free to plunge together into the baptism of fire. Yet this theory ignores the facts – the fact, for example, that women have traditionally had a larger stake in love and marriage than men, and that society expects the sexual relationship to be a woman's principal mode of self-definition. Clara tells Paul that she feels as if she has been asleep all her adult life;[84] but instead of helping her to wake up, Paul consigns her to further unconsciousness. At one point in the novel he says, 'To be rid of our individuality, which is our will, which is our effort – to live effortless, a kind of conscious sleep – that is very beautiful, I think.'[85] In one sense Paul's rejection of the double standard is a radical gesture, but on the other hand it displays considerable insensitivity to the real position of women in society. Talking of the fact that Clara's husband is living openly with another woman, Miriam says to Paul:

> 'Don't you think a position like that is hard on a woman?'
> 'Rottenly hard!'
> 'It's so unjust!' said Miriam. 'The man does as he likes –'
> 'Then let the woman also,' he said.
> 'How can she? And if she does, look at her position!'
> 'What of it?'
> 'Why, it's impossible! You don't understand what a woman forfeits –'
> 'No, I don't. But if a woman's got nothing but her fair fame to feed on, why, it's thin tack, and a donkey would die of it!'[86]

At times it almost seems as though feminism must be kept in the background of the novel as much as possible because continual reference to it would remind the reader that the sexes are *not* equally placed in society, and this in turn would upset Paul's theory of sexuality.

Clara's return to her husband at the end of the novel is singled out by Kate Millett as a particularly glaring example of *Sons and Lovers'* anti-feminism.

> Returning her to her husband, Paul even finds it convenient to enter into one of Lawrence's Blutbruderschaft bonds with Baxter Dawes, arranging an assignation in the country where Clara, meek as a sheep, is delivered over to the man she hated and left years before. The text makes it clear that Dawes had beat and deceived his wife. Yet, with a consummate emotional manipulation, Paul manages to impose his own version of her marriage on Clara, finally bringing her to say that its failure was her fault. Paul, formerly her pupil in sexuality, now imagines he has relieved Clara of what he smugly describes as the 'femme incomprise' quality which had driven her to the errors of feminism. We are given to understand that through the sexual instruction of this novice, Clara was granted feminine 'fulfillment'. Paul is now pleased to make a gift of Clara to her former owner fancying, that as the latter has degenerated through illness and poverty (Paul has had Dawes fired) he ought to be glad of salvaging such a brotherly castoff.[87]

As usual in Millett's criticism, there is much of a certain kind of truth in this savage account of the end of the novel. But the text also makes it clear that Clara has never really abandoned her commitment to Baxter. She refuses to divorce him, and 'in some way . . . she held herself still as Mrs Dawes'.[88] It is clear that this is because in the relationship with Baxter, he is the dependent one, he needs her, and she is therefore in control. When Paul asks her about her husband, 'Do you feel as if you belonged to him?', she replies, 'No . . . I think he belongs to me.'[89] Like Miriam, Clara will not, in the last issue, submit to Paul, will not choose the relationship in which she would have to be the subordinate partner.

> She did not love Dawes, never had loved him; but she believed he loved her, at least depended on her . . . She had received her confirmation; but she never believed that her life belonged to Paul Morel, nor his to her . . . They would have to part sooner or later. Even if they married, and were faithful to each other, still he would have to leave her, go on alone, and she would only have to attend to

him when he came home. But it was not possible. Each wanted a mate to go side by side with.[90]

This account of the dissolution of her affair with Paul seems to me convincing enough. The real blow to feminism in *Sons and Lovers* lies in Lawrence's failure to connect the personal world of individual development to the larger material forces which have a part in shaping it. Because it has no anchor in the material world, Clara's feminism comes to seem merely an extraneous detail, as though Lawrence had given her a squint. The personal world of feeling is explored so well in *Sons and Lovers* that we are liable to forget that there is any other; that, although we see Clara at work, we never see her 'talking on platforms' or doing any of the other things that we are assured she takes part in as a suffragist.

The emphasis on individualism in *Sons and Lovers* is also found in *The Rainbow*, which owes much in a general way to the women's movement. 'The driving force behind Ursula's efforts is, of course, the feminist movement, at its height during the years of *The Rainbow*, and a great force in Lawrence's time, one which he was compelled to deal with.'[91] But the type of feminism represented by the suffrage movement is specifically rejected.

The chapter entitled 'Shame', which describes Ursula's relationship with her teacher, Winifred, was the episode singled out by the prosecution to obtain the suppression of the novel in 1915. It is generally accepted that this chapter was a late addition to *The Rainbow*, which brings it closer to Lawrence's most intense period of speculation on homosexuality in 1915-16.[92] Of course, Lawrence had shown an interest in portraying homosexual feelings as early as *The White Peacock*; and the theme recurs in the intimacy between Paul and Baxter Dawes in *Sons and Lovers*, and later in *Aaron's Rod, Kangaroo* and *The Plumed Serpent*. But it was while Lawrence was in Cornwall that the main burst of interest in homosexuality occurred, with the composition of the final version of *Women in Love* and its suppressed prologue, and a philosophical treatise called *Goats and Compasses*, which according to Cecil Gray was mainly about homosexuality, but which Lawrence destroyed in 1917.[93] The chapter 'Shame' is Lawrence's only explicit treatment of female homosexuality.

This treatment is, however, derivative. The crux of the relationship comes in two bathing scenes, one during a school swimming lesson, the other during an evening spent at Winifred's country cottage when she and Ursula swim naked in the river. Bathing scenes were a favourite, almost a hackneyed, theme of male homosexual writers and artists, especially those celebrating the relationship between an older man, often a teacher, and his younger protégé.[94] Such relationships were often advocated for their educational value, for the unique chance that an intimate friendship gave for a responsible older man to shape the life of a young boy. Edward Carpenter, for example, declared that homosexual attachments in schools should be positively encouraged:

> It is evident that the first unfolding of a strong attachment in boyhood or girlhood must have a profound influence, while if it occurs between an elder and a younger school-mate, or — as sometimes happens — between the young thing and its teacher, its importance in the educational sense can hardly be over-rated.[95]

If Lawrence read *The Intermediate Sex* at the beginning of the war, as Emile Delavenay suggests,[96] he would have found such arguments set out there in the chapter entitled 'Affection in Education', and may have incorporated them into *The Rainbow* at a late stage — because what he seems to have done in the Winifred Inger episode is to take elements of this male homosexual tradition and transfer them to the relationship between a young girl and her teacher. (He had already, of course, used the bathing tradition in *The White Peacock*.) The title of the *Rainbow* chapter, 'Shame', was a very common euphemism for homosexual love of this kind.[97]

Many critics ignore this episode or treat it very perfunctorily, and it is true that its place in the structure of the novel is not very clear. It comes between Ursula's two experiences with Skrebensky and immediately before her entry into 'the man's world', and we are given to understand that the relationship with Winifred and the visit to Wiggiston are the real occasions of her growing up. Ursula, however, cuts the experience off from the rest of her life — 'That was a sort of secret sideshow to her life, never to be opened. She did not even think of it. It was the closed door she had not the strength to open'[98] — and this is also how the episode appears in the novel, as a self-contained section which is more or less forgotten later.

Lawrence tells us that Winifred is corrupt, and critics have for the most part taken him at his word and fitted her into the scheme of the novel accordingly. Yet at the opening of the chapter, Ursula's perception of her is entirely free from any taint of the perversity or corruption with which she later comes to be associated. Winifred is beautiful, fearless, clean, fine, clever, graceful and proud. Ursula loves

The Suffragist 39

her because she is 'proud and free as a man, yet exquisite as a woman'.[99] She is educated, emancipated and athletic. Her relationship with Ursula is obviously of the educational type praised by Carpenter. Winifred's influence is crucial in widening Ursula's circle of experience and spurring her entry into the 'man's world'. Together Winifred and Ursula demystify religion — a process that the adolescent Lawrence went through himself — and Winifred introduces Ursula to

> various women and men, educated, unsatisfied people, who still moved within the smug provincial society as if they were nearly as tame as their outward behaviour showed, but who were inwardly raging and mad.
> It was a strange world the girl was swept into, like a chaos, like the end of the world.[100]

This is very like the world of *Women in Love* — a foretaste, as it were, of that *dies irae* in which Ursula is later to participate and in which Birkin moves, affecting, like Winifred's friends, to be perfectly commonplace. Winifred also initiates Ursula into a different aspect of her female heritage from that of the uninterrupted domesticity and childbearing of her mother. 'Miss Inger was telling Ursula of a friend, how she had died in childbirth, and what she had suffered; then she told of a prostitute, and of some of her experiences with men.'[101] Many of the ideas which Winifred communicates to Ursula are close to Lawrence's own views.

> The men will do no more, — they have lost the capacity for doing . . . They fuss and talk, but they are really inane. They make everything fit into an old, inert idea. Love is a dead idea to them. They don't come to one and love one, they come to an idea, and they say 'You are my idea,' so they embrace themselves. As if I were any man's idea! As if I exist because a man has an idea of me! As if I will be betrayed by him, lend him my body as an instrument for his idea, to be a mere apparatus of his dead theory. But they are too fussy to be able to act; they are all impotent, they can't *take* a woman. They come to their own idea every time, and take that. They are like serpents trying to swallow themselves because they are hungry.[102]

From the same period one might compare Lawrence's outburst to Bertrand Russell in a letter of 12 February 1915: 'The ordinary

Englishman of the educated class goes to a woman now to masterbate [sic] himself. Because he is not going for discovery or new connection or progression, but only to repeat upon himself a known reaction.'[103]

But Winifred obviously stands condemned in some sense, and not simply for her homosexual relationship with Ursula. It is true that one of the most frequent accusations levelled at suffragists and other feminists was that they were man-hating lesbians, and some of this emerges in fictional treatments of the women's movement, such as *The Bostonians*. It seems to have been an inevitable reaction to the phenomenon of female solidarity or of women consciously choosing to remain single, and while organisations like the WSPU did their best to combat it in the interests of their public image, by emphasising the happily married lives of most of their supporters, it has been suggested that the women's movement did contribute towards a greater acceptance of female homosexuality. One commentator writes that 'it was from some secret yearning to recover the wisdom of women that the homosexual movement first manifested itself, in 1912, among the suffragettes', adding obligingly, 'it was not perverse'.[104] Edward Carpenter thought it necessary and inevitable that the women's movement should create strong personal ties between women:

> The movement among women towards their own liberation and emancipation, which is taking place all over the civilised world, has been accompanied by a marked development of the homogenic passion among the female sex. It may be said that a certain strain in the relations between the opposite sexes which has come about owing to a growing consciousness among women that they have been oppressed and unfairly treated by men, and a growing unwillingness to ally themselves unequally in marriage — that this strain has caused the womenkind to draw more closely together and to cement alliances of their own. But whatever the cause may be it is pretty certain that such comrade-alliances — and of quite devoted kind — are becoming increasingly common, and especially perhaps among the more cultured classes of women, who are working out the great cause of their sex's liberation; nor is it difficult to see the importance of such alliances in such a campaign.[105]

Lawrence, of course, concentrated his attention on male homosexual relationships, and does not appear at any time to have envisaged a real role for sisterhood, but Winifred's homosexuality does not seem to be explicitly disapproved of. His attitude is, of course, notoriously ambiguous, and he seems determined, in the matter of homosexuality, to have his cake and eat it too. As Jeffrey Meyers points out, throughout Lawrence's work 'homosexual lovers . . . are portrayed as perverse and corrupt . . . Yet the homosexuality . . . is described as nourishing and life-enhancing, and represents a meaningful and valuable relationship'.[106]

The marriage between Winifred and Ursula's Uncle Tom seems to be intended to emphasise the connection between two sets of values which Lawrence saw as equally corrupt because equally committed to the mechanical. In Tom Brangwen's case this is obvious enough, for the industrial squalor of Wiggiston and the effect on its inhabitants are condoned, if not actually caused, by him. In this respect he has affinities with Gerald in *Women in Love* and the two men share, along with Skrebensky, similar attitudes to marriage: 'He would let the machinery carry him'.[107] But the verdict on Winifred comes as something of a surprise.

> She too, Winifred, worshipped the impure abstraction, the mechanisms of matter. There, there, in the machine, in service of the machine, was she free from the clog and degradation of human feeling. There, in the monstrous mechanism that held all matter, living or dead, in its service, did she achieve her consummation and her perfect unison, her immortality.[108]

This type of writing is arguably Lawrence at his worst, but it is difficult to resist the conclusion that it is Winifred's commitment to a reformist feminism which contributes to this rather brutal dismissal of her.

The point is made rather more simply in the account of Ursula's friendship with Maggie Schofield, who helps her through the difficult early stages of her teaching career. Under Maggie's guidance she attends suffrage meetings in Nottingham and reads books such as Olive Schreiner's *Woman and Labour*. But Ursula breaks away from 'that form of life wherein Maggie must remain enclosed';[109] an 'enclosedness' which, again, seems to be associated with a particular type of feminism.

> Maggie was a great suffragette, trusting in the vote. To Ursula the vote was never a reality. She had within her the strange, passionate knowledge of religion and living far transcending the limits of the automatic system that contained the vote. But her fundamental, organic knowledge had as yet to take form and rise to utterance.

For her, as for Maggie, the liberty of woman meant something real and deep.[110]

The position here is familiar. The contrast is between the automatic or mechanical (Maggie's way, the vote, constitutional reform) and the organic (Ursula's way, individual liberation, left vague and undefined). Ursula's rejection of Maggie's narrow political feminism (Maggie has other signs of crankiness, such as a liking for vegetarian food) places her firmly in a tradition of heroines who seek something at once wider and more personal than mere political enfranchisement or reform.

Ursula's friendships with women in the feminist movement diminish in importance as the novel progresses. The last such woman to be depicted, Dorothy Russell, is reduced to the level of the caricature suffragette:

> Dorothy lived with a maiden aunt in Nottingham, and spent her spare moments slaving for the Women's Social and Political Union. She was quiet and intense, with an ivory face and dark hair looped plain over her ears. Ursula was very fond of her, but afraid of her. She seemed so old and so relentless towards herself.[111]

We are back with the 'straight-haired goggle of a girl' whom Lettie mocks in *The White Peacock*.

Critics have been known to fall into the error of confusing suffragism with feminism, and some discussions of Lawrence and feminism do not go beyond the characters mentioned in this chapter. This is a pity, for in the main the treatment of suffragists in Lawrence's work is predictable, and he has little to offer in the way of original insights into the effect of the suffrage movement on people's lives. Lawrence was consistent in his antipathy to reformist politics, and although feminism in its widest sense obviously had a bearing on some of those aspects of the relationship between the sexes in which he was so intensely interested, the suffrage movement was careful to keep its campaign to public issues. We should not expect, then, to find in his writing much sympathy with suffragism *per se*, and the presentation of suffragists in his work follows a conventional pattern in its rejection of reform in favour of individual liberation and development. Lawrence differed from other novelists of the period not in his treatment of this theme, but in the language which he created for the portrayal of such development.

Notes

1. *Votes for Women*, 29 October 1909, p. 77.
2. Margaret Llewelyn Davies (ed.), *Life As We Have Known It, by Co-operative Working Women* (Hogarth Press, London, 1931), p. x.
3. Edward Nehls (ed.), *D.H. Lawrence: A Composite Biography* (3 vols., University of Wisconsin Press, Madison, 1957-9), vol. 1, p. 135.
4. Ibid.
5. Ibid., p. 553.
6. 'E.T.', *D.H. Lawrence: A Personal Record* (Jonathan Cape, London, 1935), pp. 169-70.
7. Ibid., p. 120.
8. Nehls, *D.H. Lawrence*, vol. 1, p. 50.
9. Helen Corke, *In Our Infancy* (Cambridge University Press, Cambridge, 1975), p. 206.
10. *Letters*, vol. 1, p. 123.
11. Ibid., p. 277.
12. An article by her on 'Woman-Hating School-Masters' appeared in the *Sunday Express*, 19 April 1925.
13. Grant Allen, *The Woman Who Did* (John Lane, London, 1895), p. 8.
14. H.G. Wells, *Ann Veronica* (Fisher Unwin, London, 1909), p. 248.
15. Ibid., p. 147.
16. Sheila Rowbotham, *Women, Resistance and Revolution* (Allen Lane, London, 1972), p. 12.
17. The *Freewoman*, subtitled at first 'A Weekly Feminist Review' and later 'A Weekly Humanist Review', ran from 23 November 1911 to 10 October 1912. The *New Freewoman*, subtitled 'An Individualist Review', ran from 15 June to 15 December 1913 and subsequently became the *Egoist*.
18. *New Freewoman*, 15 June 1913, pp. 3-5.
19. Ibid., 15 August 1913, p. 81.
20. Ibid., 15 July 1913, p. 41.
21. *Freewoman*, 11 July 1912, p. 147; *New Freewoman*, 1 September 1913, p. 113. Lawrence published his poem 'Eloi, Eloi, Lama Sabachthani?' in the Imagist number of the *Egoist* (1 May 1915, pp. 75-6).
22. *New Freewoman*, 15 December 1913, p. 244.
23. *Phoenix*, p. 404.
24. Ibid., p. 405.
25. Ibid., p. 406.
26. Ibid., p. 405.
27. Ibid.
28. Ibid., p. 406.
29. Ibid., p. 405.
30. *Blast*, 20 June 1914, p. 151.
31. *The White Peacock*, p. 335.
32. Ibid., p. 337.
33. Ibid.
34. Ibid., p. 361.
35. *Sons and Lovers*, pp. 207-8.
36. Ibid., pp. 89-90.
37. Ibid., p. 90.
38. Ibid. Cf. 'Sometimes my husband rather resented the teachings of the Guild . . . The Guild, he said, was making women think too much of themselves' (Davies, *Life As We Have Known It*, p. 48).
39. John Goode, 'D.H. Lawrence' in Bernard Bergonzi (ed.), *The Twentieth Century* (History of Literature in the English Language vol. 7, Barrie and Jenkins,

London, 1970), p. 119.
40. *Sons and Lovers*, p. 40.
41. Ibid., p. 58.
42. Ibid., p. 66.
43. Emile Delavenay, *D.H. Lawrence: L'Homme et la Genèse de son Œuvre* (2 vols., Librarie C. Klincksieck, Paris, 1969), vol. 2, p. 671.
44. Letter to Blanche Jennings, 13 May 1908. *Letters*, vol. 1, p. 53.
45. Delavenay, *D.H. Lawrence: L'Homme et la Genèse de son Œuvre*, vol. 2, p. 671.
46. Ibid., vol. 2, p. 703.
47. *Sons and Lovers*, p. 317.
48. Ibid., p. 323.
49. Kate Millett, *Sexual Politics* (Hart-Davis, London, 1971), p. 254.
50. *Sons and Lovers*, p. 237.
51. Ibid.
52. Ibid.
53. Ibid.
54. Ibid., p. 238.
55. Ibid., p. 240.
56. Ibid., p. 286.
57. In 1923 Margaret Bondfield became one of the first women MPs and in 1929 the first woman cabinet member.
58. *Sons and Lovers*, p. 287.
59. Charles Rossman, ' "You are the Call and I am the Answer": D.H. Lawrence and Women', *D.H. Lawrence Review*, vol. 8, no. 3 (1975), p. 266.
60. *Sons and Lovers*, p. 287.
61. Ibid.
62. Ibid., pp. 289-90.
63. Ibid., p. 153.
64. Ibid., p. 325.
65. Ibid., p. 290. White, green and purple were the WSPU colours.
66. Ibid., p. 291.
67. Ibid., p. 321.
68. Ibid., p. 320.
69. Ibid., p. 321.
70. Ibid., p. 293.
71. Ibid., p. 294.
72. Ibid., pp. 377-8.
73. Ibid., p. 335.
74. Ibid., p. 346.
75. Ibid., p. 352.
76. Ibid., p. 346.
77. Ibid., p. 381.
78. Ibid., p. 421.
79. Ibid., my emphasis.
80. Ibid., pp. 420-1.
81. Ibid., p. 421.
82. Ibid., p. 422.
83. Ibid., p. 428.
84. Ibid., p. 334.
85. Ibid., p. 349.
86. Ibid., p. 380.
87. Millett, *Sexual Politics*, pp. 254-5.
88. *Sons and Lovers*, p. 428.
89. Ibid., p. 427.

90. Ibid., pp. 428-9.
91. Millett, *Sexual Politics*, p. 261.
92. See Mark Kinkead-Weekes, 'The Marble and the Statue: The Exploratory Imagination of D.H. Lawrence' in Maynard Mack and Ian Gregor (eds.), *Imagined Worlds* (Methuen, London, 1968), pp. 379 and 415.
93. Cecil Gray, *Peter Warlock: A Memoir of Philip Heseltine* (Jonathan Cape, London, 1934), p. 114.
94. See Timothy d'Arch Smith, *Love in Earnest* (Routledge and Kegan Paul, London, 1970), pp. 169-72, and Paul Fussell, *The Great War and Modern Memory* (Oxford University Press, London, 1975), p. 301.
95. Edward Carpenter, *The Intermediate Sex* (Swan Sonnenschein, London, 1908), p. 84.
96. Emile Delavenay, *D.H. Lawrence and Edward Carpenter* (Heinemann, London, 1971), p. 37.
97. d'Arch Smith, *Love in Earnest*, p. 31.
98. *The Rainbow*, p. 457.
99. Ibid., p. 384.
100. Ibid., p. 390.
101. Ibid., p. 386.
102. Ibid., p. 390.
103. *Letters*, vol. 2, p. 285.
104. George Dangerfield, *The Strange Death of Liberal England* (Constable, London, 1936), p. 142.
105. Carpenter, *The Intermediate Sex*, pp. 77-8.
106. Jeffrey Meyers, 'D.H. Lawrence and Homosexuality' in Stephen Spender (ed.), *D.H. Lawrence: Novelist, Poet, Prophet* (Weidenfeld and Nicolson, London, 1973), p. 136.
107. *The Rainbow*, p. 400.
108. Ibid., p. 398.
109. Ibid., p. 462.
110. Ibid., p. 456.
111. Ibid., p. 482.

2 THE DREAMING WOMAN

Much closer to Lawrence's personal concerns at this time was a type of New Woman whom he referred to variously as the 'dreaming', 'spiritual' or 'Pre-Raphaelite' woman. Feminism and Pre-Raphaelitism seem, for a variety of reasons, to have been linked in the popular imagination; at the very least, the Pre-Raphaelite woman, with her loose romantic clothes and unbound hair and air of *taedium vitae*, represented a radical challenge both to the innocent young lady of Edwardian convention and to the stereotype of the mannish suffragette. The heroine of Grant Allen's *The Woman Who Did*, for example, is explicitly portrayed as a Pre-Raphaelite type:

> She was tall and dark, with abundant black hair, richly waved above the ample forehead; and she wore a curious oriental-looking navy-blue robe of some soft woollen stuff, that fell in natural folds and set off to the utmost the lissom grace of her rounded figure. It was a sort of sleeveless sack, embroidered in front with arabesques in gold thread, and fastened obliquely two inches below the waist with a belt of gilt braid and a clasp of Moorish jewel-work. Beneath it, a bodice of darker silk showed at the arms and neck, with loose sleeves in keeping. The whole costume, though quite simple in style . . . was charming in its novelty, charming too in the way it permitted the utmost liberty and variety of movement to the lithe limbs of its wearer.[1]

The novel's cover was designed by Aubrey Beardsley. This is a typical example of the way in which the Pre-Raphaelite woman and the New Woman were linked in the sphere of design; for example, Sylvia Pankhurst, a pupil of Walter Crane at Manchester Art School, inherited a Pre-Raphaelite style which set the visual tone of the WSPU, and the bound volumes of *Votes for Women* in their purple and green covers look more like a decadence periodical than a suffragist magazine.

There was also an element in turn-of-the-century feminism which was sympathetic to the essentially spiritual and mystical representation of women which characterised Pre-Raphaelite art. There was a strong tendency in some feminist circles to emphasise women's traditional wisdom and mystical powers. Charlotte Despard, the leader of the

Women's Freedom League, perhaps best represented this trend among the official feminist organisations.

> A woman of considerable wit and natural authority, her popularity and her fame were enhanced by a superbly striking physical presence . . . Her long, startlingly pale face gave her the look of a benevolent witch, and her brilliantly white hair was always surrounded by a black-lace mantilla. A long, flowing, priestly black gown and slender feet shod in sandals completed an unusual and arresting exterior.[2]

Mrs Despard viewed materialism and spiritual darkness, rather than specific discrimination, as the principal enemies of feminism. Women's spiritual superiority to men was a convention which had been used to restrict their role to that of domestic and family life, denying them access to education and independence. Feminists to some extent adopted this convention and turned it to their own ends. The emphasis on spirituality could lead to a demand, not for sexual liberation, but for a transformation of sex from the ugly, bestial activity to which men had reduced it, to a new expression of what was essentially a spiritual relationship. Olive Schreiner, for example, asserted that 'sex and the sexual relation between man and woman have distinct æsthetic, intellectual and spiritual functions and ends',[3] and strongly denied that the women's movement was moving in the direction of sexual laxity or promiscuity. The abolition of the sexual double standard should involve a raising of the moral standard of men to the level demanded of women, not a lowering of women's standards to those of men. (In its most extreme form, this line of thought could lead to the position of Christabel Pankhurst's *The Great Scourge and How to End it* (1913), which advised women to remain celibate, as most men not only suffered from venereal disease but were in any case so perverted that intercourse with virtuous women did not satisfy them.) Unfortunately, the Pre-Raphaelite image frequently laid itself open to misinterpretation in this respect. The loose garments, the dropping of a false 'innocence', the readiness to enter into *spiritual* intimacy with men, were all too often misread as indications of sexual accessibility.

A grasp of the complex and often contradictory elements which made up this concept of the New Woman is necessary for an appreciation of a persistent theme in Lawrence's early work — the attempt to come to terms with the 'dreaming woman'. These women are emancipated, educated and intelligent; they are stimulating companions and are often crucial in the spiritual development of the men with whom they are involved; but they cannot, or will not, satisfy these men's sexual desires.

The literary paradigm is of course Sue Bridehead in Hardy's *Jude the Obscure* (1895). Reviewing the novel, Edmund Gosse wrote that 'the *vita sexualis* of Sue' was its 'central interest',[4] and the character of Sue still has the power to disturb. Hardy was attacked for his portrayal of Sue on two counts: first, her opposition to the social institution of marriage; second, her attitude towards sex, which was condemned as coquetry. Mrs Oliphant wrote of Sue that she 'makes virtue vicious by keeping the physical facts of one relationship in life in constant prominence by denying, as Arabella does by satisfying them',[5] while the *Fortnightly Review*'s critic, more bluntly, called Sue 'a flirt in the worst sense of the term'.[6] The reviewers were obviously unhappy with a heroine whose chastity sprang not from ignorance or innocence, which a legal husband might rightfully hope to dispel, but from a conscious sense of her own sexual autonomy. In a letter to Gosse written in 1895, Hardy explained that

> one of her reasons for fearing the marriage ceremony is that she fears it wd be breaking faith with Jude to withhold herself at pleasure, or altogether, after it; though while uncontracted she feels at liberty to yield herself as seldom as she chooses.[7]

There was also another reaction to the portrayal of Sue; in the preface to the 1912 edition of the novel Hardy describes the response of a German reviewer who had informed him that Sue was

> the first delineation in fiction of the woman who was coming into notice in her thousands every year — the woman of the feminist movement — the slight, pale 'bachelor' girl — the intellectualized, emancipated bundle of nerves that modern conditions were producing, . . . who does not recognize the necessity for most of her sex to follow marriage as a profession.[8]

However, neither 'feminist' nor 'flirt' adequately defines Sue. Her withholding of her sexuality comes close at times to conventional prudery. Robert B. Heilman has noted how 'her view of herself as a supra-sexual holder of prerogative and of [Jude] as a mere seeker of "gratification" is quite Victorian' and how the piquancy and complexity of her character depend on her being 'the special outsider on the one hand and . . . quite conventional on the other'. The key is the ambiguity of her 'spirituality'.

> Deliberately or instinctively Hardy is using certain Romantic values as a critical instrument against those of his own day, a free spirit against an oppressive society, the ethereal against commonplace and material. But a very odd thing happens: in conceiving of Sue as 'spirit,' and then letting her develop logically in such terms, he finds her coming up with a strong aversion to sex — in other words, with a strong infusion of the very Victorianism that many of her feelings and intellectual attitudes run counter to.[9]

This analysis applies equally to Lawrence's 'dreaming women'. In other aspects of their lives, 'spirituality' is potentially radical and liberating; but with sexuality it coincides, in effect if not in cause, with the prevailing social conventions. Not surprisingly, *Jude the Obscure* became a crucial text for Lawrence in the early stages of his writing career. The women with whom he was involved — Jessie Chambers, Helen Corke, Louie Burrows — were teachers, as Sue was training to be. They were exceptional women, educated and independent. Yet they seemed to him to be blind to his sexual needs. In the case of Helen Corke the echoes of Hardy's novel become eerily loud, for her lover had committed suicide just as Sue's undergraduate had done; an early version of Lawrence's poem 'Passing Visit to Helen' is entitled 'And Jude the Obscure and his Beloved'.

At the very outset of his writing career Lawrence was also involved with a woman who epitomised 'Pre-Raphaelite' feminism, the poet Rachel Annand Taylor. He was introduced to her at a literary gathering during 1910 and in September of that year he entered into a correspondence with her on the subject of a lecture which he was to give on her poetry to a Croydon literary society. She reinforced, from the woman's point of view, conclusions about 'spiritual women' which he was already formulating. He derived the phrase 'dreaming woman' from her, and she bequeathed him a vocabulary — of the witch, the priestess, the prophetess — which he came increasingly to use in his work. In the preface to *The Hours of Fiammetta* (1910), Rachel Annand Taylor writes of the 'two great traditions of womanhood':

> One presents the Madonna brooding over the mystery of motherhood; the other, more confusedly, tells of the acolyte, the priestess, the clairvoyante of the unknown gods. This latter exists complete in herself, a personality as definite and as significant as a symbol. She is

behind all the processes of art, though she rarely becomes a conscious artist, except in delicate and impassioned modes of living. Indeed, matters are cruelly complicated for her if the entanglements of destiny drag her forward into the deliberate æsthetic effort. Strange, wistful, bitter and sweet, she troubles and quickens the soul of man, as earthly or as heavenly lover redeeming him from the spiritual sloth which is more to be dreaded than any kind of pain.

The second tradition of womanhood does not perish; but, in these present confusions of change, women of the more emotional and imaginative type are less potent than they have been and will be again. They appear equally inimical and heretical to the opposing camps of hausfrau and of suffragist.[10]

Rachel Annand Taylor's poems embody a feminism based on women's spiritual superiority to men and their privileged function as keepers of mysteries. In 'Art and Women' she claims that women are 'nearer to the gods than poets are' because of their closeness to the natural rhythms and ancient symbols which are the basis of all art.

> For with the silver moons we wax and wane,
> And with the roses love most woundingly,
> And, wrought from flower to fruit with dim rich pain,
> The Orchard of the Pomegranates are we.[11]

The sonnet sequence which makes up *The Hours of Fiammetta* is framed by the 'Prologue of the Dreaming Women' and the 'Epilogue of the Dreaming Women'. The Prologue describes the special role of such women —

> We carry spices to the gods.
> For this we are wrought curiously,
> All vain desire and reverie . . .[12]

— while the Epilogue rejects the suffragists' demands for 'armour', 'justice', 'orb and sceptre', and asks instead that woman's sacred function as priestess and prophetess be restored.[13] The published text of Lawrence's lecture on Rachel Annand Taylor[14] betrays an uncertainty about her Pre-Raphaelite pretensions which reveals itself in irony, but the full extent of her impact upon him can be seen in the letters he sent her during 1910-11, and the degree to which her style informs much of his writing.

In *The White Peacock*, his first novel, Lawrence circles around the theme of the dreaming woman without ever quite tackling it directly. Helen Corke complains with justice that Lawrence is not interested in the female characters of the novel as individuals. 'He sees them only in relation to their men. "Take," he would seem to say to his reader, "a male creature! We shall now study its reactions to these various forms of feminine stimuli." '[15] *The White Peacock* is a self-consciously literary production, somewhat overloaded with references to Nietzsche, Schopenhauer, Wagner, Maeterlinck, George Moore, Beardsley and the Pre-Raphaelites.[16] The women in the novel are seen in terms of this literature and art (one critic has described Lettie as an '1890's belle dame sans merci')[17] and one of Lawrence's major preoccupations in the novel is to explore the implications of the concept of the Pre-Raphaelite woman. The descriptions of Lettie's appearance establish her affinity with the Pre-Raphaelite type. She has modelled herself on Sarah Bernhardt, and we see her dressed in the Symbolists' favourite colours of purple and green. Like Janey Morris and the other Pre-Raphaelite models, she is very tall, 'nearly six feet in height', and this characteristic also links her to Beardsley's elongated figures.

Lettie is also presented as a New Woman. She has been to College, gives vent to 'many banalities concerning men, and love, and marriage', and reads 'all things that dealt with modern woman'.[18] Her discontent is occasionally articulated: 'it's always the woman bears the burden';[19] 'if I were a man I would go out west and be free'.[20] After her marriage she is interested for a while in socialism and feminism and joins the Women's League. But her interest is sporadic and undirected, springing from a vague dissatisfaction that has never been analysed. Neither Leslie nor George is interested in this side of Lettie; Leslie is portrayed as a hopeless reactionary, while George infects her with his own cynicism concerning reform.

Lettie's characterisation as a Pre-Raphaelite woman may seem to be simply an attempt to add interest by presenting a fashionable and slightly controversial stereotype. But something of what Lawrence is trying to imply can be seen by looking at the gamekeeper Annable's narrative to Cyril in Chapter 11. Here some of Lawrence's lifelong obsessions can be seen in embryo. Annable reveals that he was formerly a parson, who fell in love with a titled lady. Lady Crystabel is also a New Woman; she is 'very fine and frank and unconventional'. 'She said we were in the wilderness and could do as we liked. She made me wear flannels and soft clothes.'[21] The marriage, however, is not a success:

She wouldn't have children — no, she wouldn't — said she daren't. That was the root of the difference at first. But she cooled down, and if you don't know the pride of my body you'd never know my humiliation. I tried to remonstrate — and she looked simply astounded at my cheek. I never got over that amazement.

She began to get souly. A poet got hold of her, and she began to affect Burne-Jones — or Waterhouse — it was Waterhouse — she was a lot like one of his women — Lady of Shalott, I believe. At any rate, she got souly, and I was her animal — *son animal* — *son boeuf*. I put up with that for above a year. Then I got some servants' clothes and went.[22]

For Annable, the essence of Lady Crystabel seems to be represented by the peacock with its screeching voice, which fouls the statue of an angel in the churchyard. 'A woman to the end, I tell you, all vanity and screech and defilement.'[23] A connection with Lettie is obviously intended; she is several times described wearing feathers, and her relationship with George is a sort of parallel to that of Lady Crystabel and Annable. The manuscript version of the novel is more explicit about the peacock image; a woman defiles the 'angel' in a man by refusing to recognise his sexual need.[24] The significance of the Beardsley drawings becomes clearer here. They excite George to a keen physical desire for Lettie — but ironically the drawings themselves are of women notorious for arousing desire but not satisfying it, Salome and Atalanta. And Beardsley, of course, shows Salome dressed in peacock skirts or surrounded by groups of peacocks. Lettie is also a temptress of this type:

> As she turned laughing to the two men, she let her cloak slide over her white shoulder and fall with silk splendour of a peacock's gorgeous blue over the arm of the large settee. There she stood, with her white hand upon the peacock of her cloak, where it tumbled against her dull orange dress. She knew her own splendour, and she drew up her throat laughing and brilliant with triumph.[25]

She is capable of sexual arousal but draws back from its implications. She tries to persuade Leslie into a 'spiritual' love for her, although his reaction is, 'Hang thin souls, Lettie! I'm not one of your souly sort. I can't stand Pre-Raphaelities.'[26] She also attempts to avoid her marriage with him on the grounds that 'I can't — we can't be — don't you see — oh, what do they say – flesh of one flesh.'[27]

The complex of ideas built up around this particular image of womanhood comes to include the shy, quiet Emily as well. Emily is a 'Burne-Jones damsel' and the narrator, Cyril, reproaches her for her excessive spirituality: 'Troublesome shadows are always crowding across your eyes, and you cherish them. You think the flesh of the apple is nothing, nothing. You only care for the eternal pips.'[28] There is no simple contrast, either, between Lettie and the voluptuous, sensual Meg, whom George marries in the hope that she will at least provide him with home comforts and sexual satisfaction. Emily and Meg are no different from Lettie in the aspect which matters most to the men in the novel:

> A woman is so ready to disclaim the body of a man's love; she yields him her own soft beauty with so much gentle patience and regret; she clings to his neck, to his head and his cheeks, fondling them for the soul's meaning that is there, and shrinking from his passionate limbs and body. It was with some perplexity, some anger and bitterness that I watched Emily moved almost to ecstasy by the baby's small, innocuous person.
>
> 'Meg never found any pleasure in me as she does in the kids,' said George bitterly, for himself.[29]

In *The Trespasser* Lawrence refines further his concept of the woman who can only love spiritually, not physically. Reviewers praised him for successfully anatomising in fiction the psychic *femme fatale*: 'The author of *The Trespasser* has, keenly and courageously, analysed the woman of dreams, the seeker after extreme sensations, not physical, but psychic.'[30] Lawrence says of Helena: 'She belonged to that class of "Dreaming Women" with whom passion exhausts itself at the mouth. Her desire was accomplished in a real kiss.'[31] Helena is the result of a long process of refinement, the same comment that Lawrence was later to make about Sue Bridehead in the *Study of Thomas Hardy*: 'For centuries, a certain type of woman has been rejecting the "animal" in humanity, till now her dreams are abstract, and full of fantasy, and her blood runs in bondage, and her kindness is full of cruelty.'[32] Like Lettie, she is at the centre of a tragedy which is not her fault, but which seems based on an unresolvable clash of human natures, an unbridgeable male-female dichotomy.

> The best sort of women – the most interesting – are the worst for us . . . By instinct they aim at suppressing the gross and animal in us. Then they are supersensitive – refined a bit beyond humanity

. . . She can't live without us, but she destroys us. These deep, interesting women don't want *us*; they want the flowers of the spirit they can gather of us. We, as natural men, are more or less degrading to them and to their love of us. Therefore they destroy the natural man in us — that is, us altogether.[33]

In *The Trespasser* Lawrence makes very little attempt to analyse the character of Helena. But we know from Helen Corke's own accounts of the experiences on which the novel was based that it was precisely because she felt her identity as a woman to be precarious, precisely because she had spent so much time and effort building herself a complete and self-sufficient personality out of scanty resources, that she was unwilling to sink herself in what she saw as the self-immolation of physical love. Another early reviewer said of the fictional character that 'the picture of her relations with her lover suggests deep reservations, as of a woman who cannot lose sense of her own identity even in the supreme intimacy of love'.[34] The real-life Helen had no wish to lose an identity which, as her autobiography shows, had cost her so much to establish.

Some idea of the missing dimension in *The Trespasser* can be gained if we turn to Helen Corke's own fictionalised account of her early life, *Neutral Ground*, which reveals more clearly the feminist orientation of her attitude. She gives her fictional self a 'neuter' name, Ellis. Ellis conceives an early repugnance for the limitations of motherhood which conditions her attitude to marriage: 'And never again would one be readier to jump and run than to walk, never quite free and alone, never able in all one's life to say, "To-morrow I will go out into the wide world." '[35] 'Men and women ought to be made alike,' complains Ellis. 'Women get all the pain and trouble. It's *not* fair.'[36] And later, 'I *don't* imagine myself married. I can't, somehow — it isn't natural to me.'[37] Ellis's attitude crystallises around her difference from her cousin Aileen, the conventional 'womanly' woman in the novel, who dies in childbirth; and is reinforced by her reading of Olive Schreiner's *Story of an African Farm* and her identification with its heroine, Lyndall. Her feelings about sexuality are also confirmed by the more conventional moral teaching she has received:

> The balance of Ellis's reading, and what had passed during childhood and adolescence for social experience, had taught her, in effect, that while the body, with its passions, was in necessary subjection to moral law, the mind moved above it in a state of

exalted and unchallenged freedom. With this philosophy she entered upon womanhood.[38]

In *Neutral Ground* Ellis's lover regards her detachment from sex as the 'expression of spiritual superiority',[39] but although she wants to inhabit 'a kingdom that lay serene, beyond the waves of sex contention',[40] it is not simple physical frigidity which inhibits her sexual response. 'What did he want of her? No simple physical reaction to the urgency of his body, that she might in gratitude have given him, for she loved him.'[41] Her fear is that by entering into a 'conventional' sexual relationship she will also be forced to play the other conventional roles of wife, housekeeper and mother, and she prefers not to take the risk. 'She did not want to be either Domine's housekeeper or the mother of his children.'[42]

However, Ellis regards herself as a special being, a kind of freak. Her feminism is individualistic; she does not suggest that society should change. The novel asks only 'What strange development of humanity expressed itself in her?'[43]

In reality she had no right to use her own nature as standard at all. It represented no standard, but something isolated and exceptional . . . She had lost Domine; she must lose Derrick. They were men, and their sex called to her as woman. She could not answer that call; God had not given her the answer.[44]

In Ellis's inability to extend the beginnings of her feminist analysis beyond herself, to see (as the mature Helen Corke saw in retrospect) that what really repulses her is not sexual activity itself, but its association with conventional rules and attitudes enforced by society, the inner logic of the novel falters and Ellis has no alternative but to regard herself as a misfit. She is further confirmed in this attitude by the revelation of what she takes to be her own bisexuality — her passionate attraction to her cousin Aileen as a child, and later her deep love for Derrick's fiancée Theresa (a portrait of Jessie Chambers).

Neutral Ground supplies at least an outline of the motivation behind the behaviour of the 'dreaming woman', something which is lacking in Lawrence's repeated descriptions. 'The Witch à la Mode', for example, introduces a new label but little fresh in the way of insight. The 'witch' of the title is 'intense and unnatural',[45] another dreaming woman who is satisfied with the kiss that only serves to arouse her lover: 'she wanted no more of him than that kiss'.[46] In his frustration he kicks over the lamp whose white globe seems to represent the woman's infuriating purity, but succeeds only in starting a fire which injures him while leaving her intact.

Lawrence's analysis of the weakness and failure of the 'spiritual woman' in *Sons and Lovers* was noticed by his earliest reviewers and has been commented upon by critics ever since. Louise Maunsell Field, writing in the *New York Times Book Review* in 1913, remarked, 'One must go far to find a better study of an intense woman, so over-spiritualized that she has almost lost touch with ordinary life and ordinary humanity, than [Lawrence] has given us in the person of Miriam.'[47] But *Sons and Lovers* also marks the beginning of Lawrence's realisation of the insufficiency of such labelling.

The initial descriptions of Miriam establish her affinity with the Pre-Raphaelite type. At first we are shown that Miriam perceives *herself* in this way in order to escape from the drudgery of her day-to-day life: 'She herself was something of a princess turned into a swine-girl, in her own imagination.'[48] Then we learn that this is also Paul's perception of her, so that between them they acquiesce in the creation of a shared myth about Miriam's image:

> Miriam seemed as in some dreamy tale, a maiden in bondage, her spirit dreaming in a land far away and magical. And her discoloured, old blue frock and her broken boots seemed only like the romantic rags of King Cophetua's beggar-maid.[49]

'If you put red berries in your hair,' asks Paul, 'why would you look like some witch or priestess, and never like a reveller?'[50] By such remarks Miriam is tacitly established as a 'spiritual' woman, until eventually Paul discovers that he doesn't like what he has created.

The crucial issue of the novel is once again the nature of the sexual failure between the hero and a 'dreaming woman', and this aspect has of course received much critical attention. The reader is given the impression that the failure of the relationship is predominantly Miriam's fault, despite allusions to Paul's own shortcomings. However, there is, if we read the novel carefully, more involved than simply excessive 'spirituality' on Miriam's part. Like Ellis in *Neutral Ground*, Miriam resists the yielding of identity that passion seems to demand.

The novel does contain the germ of Miriam's own side of the story. One of the incidents often ignored by commentators is the scene towards the end, when Paul's ego receives a terrific blow from the realisation that Miriam has been developing apart (and away) from him, and that he has not been her hero as he imagined. 'She had despised him when he thought she worshipped him . . . All these years she had treated him as if he were a hero, and thought of him secretly as an infant, a foolish child.'[51] Miriam has struggled to resist Paul's domination over her, and succeeded:

> She knew she felt in a sort of bondage to him, which she hated because she could not control it. She had hated her love for him from the moment it grew too strong for her. And, deep down, she had hated him because she loved him and he dominated her. She had resisted his domination. She had fought to keep herself free of him in the last issue.[52]

Running as a minor strand through the novel is Miriam's desire for independence, towards which Paul displays a marked lack of interest. In the last chapter she reveals to him that she is to become a teacher, but Paul is 'rather disappointed' and seeks to play down her achievement: 'You'll find earning your own living isn't everything.'[53] These often-ignored passages point up the inadequacy of the romantic, Pre-Raphaelite image which Paul assigns to Miriam, and such an interpretation is supported both by Jessie Chambers's account in *D.H. Lawrence: A Personal Record* and by a couple of short stories which deal with similar themes.

Jessie makes it clear that she did not see herself as a 'spiritual' woman; in her account it is Lawrence who suffers from a heavily dualistic view of body and soul, while she talks of 'my inescapable conviction that one must accept life as a whole'.[54] It was Lawrence who 'tried his utmost to persuade me that love and marriage could have no part in my life'.[55] But she rejected this obsessive labelling of her:

> Lawrence had found a new name for me. I was no longer Emily Brontë; I was a pre-Raphaelite woman. I disliked the new label even more than the old one. It made me feel that for him I was becoming less and less of a suffering, struggling human being, and more and more of a mental concept, a pure abstraction.[56]

Lawrence's own acknowledgement of the insufficiency of the Pre-Raphaelite image is evident in two short stories which seem in fact to be fantasies about Jessie. In both, the hero is shocked to find an old sweetheart, whom he had always thought of as a 'dreaming woman', unexpectedly involved with a handsome young lover. In 'A Modern

Lover' the hero goes some way towards winning the woman back to him by his intellectual conversation and sophistication, although the reunion still falters over the issue of sex. In 'The Shades of Spring' the hero returning home for a visit is a married man, but is nevertheless appalled that his former sweetheart has taken a young gamekeeper as a lover. 'He knew he had mistaken her, had taken her for something she was not . . . He was startled to see his young love, his nun, his Botticelli angel, so revealed.'[57]

Around 1915 Lawrence returns to the theme of the witch or prophetess. His attitude is now more detached, possibly because his personal sexual satisfaction is no longer at stake. This was the period when Lawrence dreamt of a social revolution followed by the establishment of a new hierarchic community in which women were to play an equal part; during the early years of the war his feeling that women must take the lead in transforming society was very strong. For a time he envisaged Ottoline Morrell as the female leader of his ideal state, and a letter written to her at the beginning of 1915 demonstrates that the concept of the seeress was now capable of winning his approval because it could embody the idea of intuition, of consciousness 'in the blood', which he was now refining.

> Why don't you have the pride of your own intrinsic self? Why must you tamper with the idea of being an ordinary physical woman — wife, mother, mistress. Primarily, you are none of these things. Primarily, you belong to a special type, a special race of women: like Cassandra in Greece, and some of the great woman saints. They were the great *media* of truth, of the deepest truth: through them, as through Cassandra, the truth came as through a fissure from the depths and the burning darkness that lies out of the depth of time. It is necessary for this great type to re-assert itself on the face of the earth. It is not the Salon lady and the blue stocking — it is not the critic and judge, but the priestess, the medium, the prophetess.[58]

The resurgence of interest in this theme may have come from the publication in 1914 of Edward Carpenter's *Intermediate Types Among Primitive Folk*, which argues that those of 'intermediate sex' are naturally prophets, seers and priests:

> I believe that the blending of the masculine and feminine temperaments would in some of these cases produce persons whose perceptions would be so subtle and complex and rapid as to come under

the head of genius, persons of intuitive mind who would perceive things without knowing how ... diviners and prophets in a very real sense.[59]

In this spirit Lawrence returned to the enigma of Sue Bridehead in his *Study of Thomas Hardy*. He now 'has sympathy for her predicament, because he sees it stored up for her by history'.[60] 'Sue is the production of the long selection by man of the woman in whom the female is subordinated to the male principle ... One of the supremest products of our civilization is Sue, and a product that well frightens us.'[61] He asks that society should have a place for Sue, who belongs 'to the old woman-type of witch or prophetess'.[62] 'Sue had a being, special and beautiful ... Why must it be assumed that Sue is an "ordinary" woman — as if such a thing existed? ... Why was there no place for her?'[63]

However, Lawrence's reading of *Jude the Obscure* also emphasises how the seemingly neat sexual parallelism of the Hardy study collapses in practice. In his account, the female characters are helplessly defined by their 'male' or 'female' labels (Arabella does not seek mental, nor Sue physical, stimulation), yet in Jude the categories 'male' and 'female' are simply names for different aspects of the human personality which both demand recognition. Women suffer in a way that men do not from Lawrence's insistence on the dichotomy between male and female, spirit and flesh. For Lawrence, a woman who is not 'physical' is no woman at all, and he necessarily sees Sue as having embraced the 'male principle', the life of the mind: 'She did not, like an ordinary woman, receive all she knew through her senses, her instincts, but through her consciousness.'[64] It is implied that, in a woman, the existence of the two sets of characteristics that Lawrence designates 'male' and 'female' can only cause conflict. Of Sue he says that, because of the 'atrophied female' in her, 'she contained always the rarest, most deadly anarchy in her own being'.[65] Lawrence's sympathy for the 'spiritual woman' is short-lived: in his statement that Sue 'felt all the time the ghastly sickness of dissolution upon her, she was as a void unto herself',[66] the germ of the reaction can be seen. The theme of dissolution is pursued in *Women in Love* and its suppressed prologue, where the same sort of imagery is used of Hermione.

The prologue to *Women in Love* is really retrogressive — a re-working of Lawrence's experiences with the old 'spiritual women', now projected onto the figure of Ottoline Morrell. It tells of how Hermione set herself to be Birkin's 'priestess' while they were both at Oxford. Her 'emptiness' and 'dissolution' are the result of her realisation that

Birkin is no god and does not deserve her worship; but she can find no function outside the role of priestess which she has created for herself — 'the spiritual woman who waited at the tomb in her sandals and her mourning robes'.[67] Like Paul and Miriam, Hermione and Birkin drag on their relationship without ever feeling able to commit themselves. Hermione is left with nothing to replace her cynicism:

> She did not believe in her own universals — they were sham. She did not believe in the inner life — it was a trick, not a reality. She did not believe in the spiritual world — it was an affectation ... She was a priestess without belief, without conviction, suckled in a creed outworn, and condemned to the reiteration of mysteries that were not divine to her.[68]

The priestess ideal is outworn, because the woman who should be a medium for intuitive truth has not found such a truth which will carry conviction, so she turns to her will, which is not the instrument, properly speaking, of the seer.

Once Lawrence had succeeded in extricating himself from his personal involvements with the various 'dreaming women', the antimaterialism and emphasis on intuition in this type of feminism did hold a brief appeal for him. But he was working his way towards a form of intuition based not on the spirit, but on the body and the instincts. The period of real, felt sympathy with feminism in Lawrence's writing career is in fact a short one, spanning only the years 1913-15, although many critics would also argue that this was the period of his best work. The interest was brought to an abrupt end by the changes in the status of women occasioned by the First World War.

Notes

1. Grant Allen, *The Woman Who Did* (John Lane, London, 1895), pp. 3-4.
2. David Mitchell, *Women on the Warpath* (Jonathan Cape, London, 1966), p. 302.
3. Olive Schreiner, *Woman and Labour* (Fisher Unwin, London, 1911), pp. 26-7.
4. Edmund Gosse, 'Mr. Hardy's New Novel', *Cosmopolis*, vol. 1, no. 1 (1896), p. 67.
5. Mrs Oliphant, 'The Anti-Marriage League', *Blackwood's Magazine*, January 1896, p. 140.
6. R.Y. Tyrrell, 'Jude the Obscure', *Fortnightly Review*, 1 June 1896, p. 860.
7. Thomas Hardy, *Collected Letters*, vol. 2, ed. Richard Little Purdy and Michael Millgate (Oxford University Press, Oxford, 1980), p. 99.

8. Thomas Hardy, *Jude the Obscure* (revised edition, Macmillan, London, 1912), pp. xi–xii.
9. Robert B. Heilman, 'Hardy's Sue Brideshead', *Nineteenth Century Fiction*, vol. 20, no. 4 (1966), p. 308.
10. Rachel Annand Taylor, *The Hours of Fiammetta* (Elkin Matthews, London, 1910), pp. 5-6.
11. Ibid., p. 48.
12. Ibid., p. 11.
13. Ibid., pp. 74–5.
14. *Phoenix II*, pp. 217–20.
15. Helen Corke, 'Concerning *The White Peacock*' in *D.H. Lawrence: The Croydon Years* (University of Texas Press, Austin, 1965), p. 52.
16. See Jeffrey Meyers, *Painting and the Novel* (Manchester University Press, Manchester, 1975), pp. 46–52, and George H. Ford, *Double Measure* (Holt, Rinehart and Winston, New York, 1965), pp. 54–5.
17. Ford, *Double Measure*, p. 55.
18. *The White Peacock*, p. 92.
19. Ibid., p. 160.
20. Ibid., p. 243.
21. Ibid., p. 176.
22. Ibid., p. 177.
23. Ibid., p. 175.
24. See Ford, *Double Measure*, p. 53.
25. *The White Peacock*, p. 292.
26. Ibid., p. 104.
27. Ibid., p. 227.
28. Ibid., p. 86.
29. Ibid., p. 317.
30. *New York Times Review of Books*, 17 November 1912, p. 677.
31. *The Trespasser*, p. 64.
32. Ibid.
33. Ibid., p. 112.
34. *Athenaeum*, 1 June 1912, p. 614.
35. Helen Corke, *Neutral Ground* (Arthur Barker, London, 1933), p. 53. Although not published until 1933 the novel was completed in 1918.
36. Ibid., p. 55.
37. Ibid., p. 95.
38. Ibid., p. 123.
39. Ibid., p. 154.
40. Ibid., p. 190.
41. Ibid., p. 293.
42. Ibid., p. 164.
43. Ibid., p. 182.
44. Ibid., pp. 285–6. 'Derrick' is Derrick Hamilton, a portrait of Lawrence.
45. *The Mortal Coil and Other Stories*, p. 102.
46. Ibid., p. 107.
47. *New York Times Review of Books*, 21 September 1913, p. 479.
48. *Sons and Lovers*, p. 191.
49. Ibid., p. 194.
50. Ibid., p. 240.
51. Ibid., pp. 360–1.
52. Ibid., p. 358.
53. Ibid., p. 487.
54. 'E.T.', *D.H. Lawrence: A Personal Record* (Jonathan Cape, London, 1935), p. 153.

55. Ibid.
56. Ibid., p. 145.
57. *The Prussian Officer and Other Stories*, pp. 125 and 127. See also A.H. Gomme, 'Jessie Chambers and Miriam Leivers' in A.H. Gomme (ed.), *D.H. Lawrence: A Critical Study of the Major Novels and Other Writings* (Harvester, Hassocks, 1978) and Louis L. Martz, 'Portrait of Miriam: A Study in the Design of *Sons and Lovers*' in Maynard Mack and Ian Gregor (eds.), *Imagined Worlds* (Methuen, London, 1968).
58. Letter to Lady Ottoline Morrell, 1 March 1915. *Letters*, vol. 2, pp. 297-8. Cassandra's fate of prophesying the truth but never being believed was inflicted on her by Apollo because she refused his sexual advances.
59. Edward Carpenter, *Intermediate Types Among Primitive Folk* (George Allen, London, 1914), p. 62.
60. Richard Swigg, *Lawrence, Hardy and American Literature* (Oxford University Press, London, 1972), p. 74.
61. *Phoenix*, pp. 496-7.
62. Ibid., p. 496.
63. Ibid., p. 510.
64. Ibid., p. 501.
65. Ibid., p. 497.
66. Ibid., p. 502.
67. *Phoenix II*, p. 95.
68. *Women in Love*, p. 373.

3 LAWRENCE, FEMINISM AND THE WAR

With an incongruous irony seldom equalled in the history of revolutions, the spectacular pageant of the woman's movement, vital and colourful with adventure, with initiative, with sacrificial emotion, crept to its quiet, unadvertised triumph in the deepest night of wartime depression.[1]

The First World War brought women the vote, the struggle for which had been the predominant symbol of feminist enterprise in the pre-war years. But the war also brought about more fundamental and spectacular changes in women's lives, some temporary, others more lasting. A highly industrialised nation faced with mass conscription of its active men had no choice but to look for an alternative labour force, and the employment of women was the obvious answer. The large-scale entry of women into the labour market did not take place overnight, and there was considerable hostility to it. But the exceptional requirements of the war economy swept aside some of the conventional notions about women's place in society. The movement of women into jobs previously held by men proved to be the crucial factor in their changing status during the war. It gave them new social freedoms and a staggering new financial independence. For example, before the war the average weekly wage for women in paid employment had been 11s 7d; but a war-time bus conductress, like those in Lawrence's story 'Tickets, Please', started on a wage of £2 5s per week.[2]

As Sheila Rowbotham has pointed out, it would be naïve to see the work in itself as particularly emancipating for women.[3] It was frequently hard, dangerous and monotonous, especially in the munitions factories which came to employ large numbers of the new female workforce. Obviously, only a small number of the women doing war-work were motivated by an overt political commitment to feminism; most wanted to do their bit to help their country, or sought escape from a repressive family or the rigours of domestic service. There was in any case no single feminist policy on the war. Emmeline and Christabel Pankhurst became fervent patriots, and there was talk of 'women's right to serve', while other women considered pacifism to be more in line with feminist principles. Although the basis for most of the social and economic changes that affected women had been laid by the pre-war feminist campaigns, when the changes actually came they were dictated more by economic necessity and the exigencies of war than by any conscious ideology. The number of women employed in industry in Britain increased by more than a million during the war, with about seven hundred thousand directly replacing men. Other women moved into a large number of other traditionally male occupations, and many whose husbands or fathers had run small businesses took these over. Others joined the new women's services such as the WAAC, or semi-official organisations like the Women's Land Army, while thousands more worked voluntarily in relief organisations. It was a remarkable show of strength by the female population which succeeded in dispelling many myths about women's role.

One of the most important by-products of the war for women was the way in which it changed attitudes to sexuality in a direction that was generally in their favour. The new freedom that women derived from war-work, and the casting aside of conventional restraints in the highly-charged emotional atmosphere of war, contributed to this. Extra-marital sexual relationships was less harshly looked upon, conventional expectations about chastity were relaxed and the unmarried mother was more sympathetically treated. An official report stated that men and women were 'so thrown into daily contact with each other that conventional notions of a certain reserve as between the sexes have been very largely modified'.[4] In such circumstances some of the repressions and taboos which had surrounded female sexuality were bound to be removed, and this shift in sexual *mores* naturally caused some alarm. A worried lady wrote towards the end of the war of 'the alarming rapidity with which the women of the country are accepting the laxer standard of morality', blaming it on 'a short-sighted system of education, the excitement inherent in war conditions, [and] the emancipation of women, immediately followed by the economic independence of very large numbers under conditions removed from home influences'.[5] There is no doubt that the war *was* an emancipating experience for most women. It changed their image of themselves, and the public's image of them, from decorative but largely useless creatures with their own sphere of trivial interests and duties, to people of resourcefulness, strength and capability who differed from men much less than had been imagined.

That the experience of the war also marked a turning-point in Lawrence's life and work has, of course, been widely acknowledged and discussed. It set him off on his 'savage pilgrimage', and, as Neil Myers has written, transformed him 'from a symbolist experimenter in the traditional novel into the compulsive, chaotic, half-comic propagandist of the popular imagination'.[6] Myers argues convincingly that the post-war Lawrence deserves as much attention as the more accessible author of *Sons and Lovers* or *The Rainbow*.

> If one takes World War I and its aftermath seriously, one must take seriously the Lawrence who spilled his awesome energy in reaction to it. One must take seriously precisely what alienates so many readers — the restless, angry disorder, and the interest in the kinds of savage energies that would fill the sudden chasm that the war had opened.[7]

In Lawrence's post-war exploration of power relationships and 'savage energies', male dominance plays a crucial part. Lawrence develops in the twenties an explicit anti-feminism which is of a different quality from the more open-ended probings of love and power to be found in his earlier work. Even in, say, *Women in Love* (written largely during the war), the notion of male supremacy is only one of a whole range of controversial subjects discussed, often in a spirit of intellectual play, by the central characters. Ultimately, the reader of *Women in Love* feels that Lawrence has no one axe to grind; in a complex presentation of possibilities and potentialities we are not forced to take sides. This poise certainly vanishes to a large extent in the post-war works, and anti-feminism, along with other notions which had earlier been only possibilities, becomes an imperative. Yet the very explicit historical relationship between the changing position of women in the war years and Lawrence's launching on his career as the prophet of male supremacy has rarely been discussed.

During the first part of the war Lawrence continued to insist on the need for women's voices to be heard and on the necessity for the feminine side of experience to be brought into prominence. A month after the outbreak of hostilities he wrote to Gordon Campbell: 'The war doesn't alter my beliefs or visions . . . I believe there is no getting of a vision, as you call it, before we get our sex right: before we get our souls fertilised by the *female*.'[8] This attitude is reflected in the emphasis on balance and relationship in the *Study of Thomas Hardy*, written around this time. In the autumn of 1915 he wrote to Cynthia Asquith, 'If only the women would get up and speak with authority.'[9]

> I very much want you to tell me what you think, because it is a question for the *women* of the land now to decide: the men will

never see it. I don't know one single man who would give the faintest response to this. But I still have some hope of the women.[10]

On the same note he wrote to Hugh Meredith, 'I can make nothing of the men, they are all dead ... Perhaps the women —.'[11] During the various stages of his war-time dabbling in revolutionary political theory with Bertrand Russell, he continued to envisage a crucial role for women in the reconstruction of the state.

It is all the more surprising, then, to discover an abrupt espousal of male supremacy which coincides with the end of the war. In a letter to Katherine Mansfield in November 1918 Lawrence writes:

> I do think a woman must yield some sort of precedence to a man, and he must take this precedence. I do think men must go ahead absolutely in front of their women, without turning round to ask for permission or approval from their women. Consequently the women must follow as it were unquestioningly.[12]

This assertion has the air of a discovery newly formulated, and Lawrence adds as if in apology, 'I can't help it, I believe this.' Frieda, he says, thinks his attitude 'antediluvian'. It was shortly after this crucial letter to Katherine Mansfield that Lawrence wrote 'Tickets, Please', 'Monkey Nuts' and 'The Fox', three stories dealing explicitly with the overturning of traditional sexual roles and relationships as a result of the war.[13] It is as if, at this time, Lawrence suddenly consolidated a whole new set of attitudes on the relationship between the sexes. What women had proved during the war was that they were capable of doing men's work and of assimilating themselves into the man's world. This was not the sort of revolution that Lawrence had hoped for: he had urged the 'feminisation' of experience, the necessity for men to take women, and the feminine side of their own natures, seriously. He had never argued that women should enter the masculine world of industry and technology which he hated. In 1917, when he was asked to write an article on the recruitment of women into traditional male occupations, Lawrence had replied that he hadn't 'the guts' to write it.

> All I can say is, that in the tearing asunder of the sexes lies the universal death, in the assuming of the male activities by the female, there takes place the horrid swallowing of her own young, by the woman ... I am sure woman will destroy man, intrinsically, in this country. But there is something in me, which stops still and

becomes dark, when I think of it ... I am sure there is some ghastly Clytemnestra victory ahead, for the women.[14]

When the war ended, the great social upheaval which Lawrence had hoped for did not materialise; rather, he found most of the things he detested about pre-war society left intact. In particular, he must have felt that the women in whom he had placed much of his hope for the future had merely become more like men. In 1914 Lawrence had written approvingly of woman 'becoming individual, self-responsible, taking her own initiative'.[15] The three stories about the war which I discuss in this chapter show a tremendous unease about the directions which that initiative had taken.

Lionel Trilling has written that 'Tickets, Please' 'exemplifies the drastic revision of the notion of womanliness'[16] which was brought about by the First World War. The story concerns a group of tram conductresses who unite to humiliate their womanising inspector, John Thomas Raynor.

> The girls are fearless young hussies. In their ugly blue uniform, skirts up to their knees, shapeless old peaked caps on their heads, they have all the *sang-froid* of an old non-commissioned officer. With a tram packed with howling colliers, roaring hymns downstairs and a sort of antiphony of obscenities upstairs, the lasses are perfectly at their ease. They pounce on the youths who try to evade their ticket-machine. They push off the men at the end of their distance. They are not going to be done in the eye — not they. They fear nobody — and everybody fears them.[17]

The presentation of the tram conductresses works on both a realistic and a symbolic level. Such women were among the élite of the new female work-force, earning over £2 a week at a time when the Lawrences could rent a Cornish cottage for £5 a year. Their fighting spirit is reflected in their pseudo-military uniforms; it was one of the great culture-shocks of the war for women to be seen in this kind of uniform, but it does give them 'all the *sang-froid* of an old non-commissioned officer'. And it is as warriors, combatants, Amazons, that they feature in this tale. Their fight is against men, or against man's representative, the phallic male himself, John Thomas. So it is apt that from the start the women are in authority over their male passengers. A tram conductor does not *serve* the public in the same way that, say, a shop assistant does, which is possibly one of the reasons why it was a traditionally male job. Having boarded the tram the passenger is obliged to pay, and the job of the conductor is almost to extort the money. So the girls 'pounce on' those who try to avoid payment, and the whole story is, on one level, a kind of extended pun on the notion of 'making men pay'.

The theme of battle is reinforced by the mock-heroic tone in which Lawrence describes Annie Stone, who leads the other women into the fight. 'She is peremptory, suspicious, and ready to hit first. She can hold her own against ten thousand. The step of that tram-car is her Thermopylae.'[18] Rejected by John Thomas for demanding more from their relationship than his mere 'nocturnal presence', Annie enlists the help of his other former sweethearts, 'the half dozen girls who knew John Thomas only too well'.[19] Trapped by the girls in a room at the depot on a Sunday evening, John Thomas is first subjected to friendly taunts and humiliating games. But the mock-heroism of the first part of the story gives way to real violence, graphically described.

> She had taken off her belt, and swinging it, she fetched him a sharp blow over the head with the buckle end. He sprang and seized her. But immediately the other girls rushed upon him, pulling and tearing and beating him. Their blood was now thoroughly up. He was their sport now. They were going to have their own back, out of him. Strange, wild creatures, they hung on him and rushed at him to bear him down. His tunic was torn right up the back, Nora had hold at the back of his collar, and was actually strangling him. Luckily the button burst. He struggled in a wild frenzy of fury and terror, almost mad terror. His tunic was simply torn off his back, his shirt-sleeves were torn away, his arms were naked. The girls rushed at him, clenched their hands on him and pulled at him: or they rushed at him and pushed him, butted him with all their might: or they struck him wild blows. He ducked and cringed and struck sideways. They became more intense.
>
> At last he was down. They rushed on him, kneeling on him. He had neither breath nor strength to move. His face was bleeding with a long scratch, his brow was bruised.[20]

The persistent theme in the attack on John Thomas is to force him to choose one of the women, to distinguish between them as individuals. But when he finally capitulates they each in turn reject him, although their renunciation costs an effort, so integral to the mythology of femininity is the dream, here parodied, of being chosen from amongst others by the handsome male.

The feeling that prevails at the end of the story is that something stupendous has happened, that things have got out of hand, that the women have gone further than they intended. By bonding together to humiliate the promiscuous male the women have indeed broken several taboos of patriarchy, and their sense of the enormity of what they have done is justified. They have attacked the double standard and their own status as sexual objects; attacked the notion that women are incapable of solidarity and must always compete with each other when a man is at stake; and shown themselves capable of violent action. It is partly because of this breaking of taboos that the story has a powerful and shocking quality. It is also Lawrence at his technical best, the build-up of tension as friendly revenge turns to actual physical assault being particularly well handled; and the various elements — realism, symbolism, mythology, psychological observation — are painlessly integrated.[21]

'Monkey Nuts' also deals with a woman in war-time taking a sexual relationship into her own hands. It concerns the relations of a landgirl, Miss Stokes, with two soldiers.

> Miss Stokes watched the two men from under her broad felt hat. She had seen hundreds of Alberts, khaki soldiers standing in loose attitudes, absorbed in watching nothing in particular. She had seen also a good many Joes, quiet, good-looking young soldiers with half-averted faces. But there was something in the turn of Joe's head, and something in his quiet, tender-looking form, young and fresh — which attracted her eye. As she watched him closely from below, he turned as if he felt her, and his dark-blue eye met her straight, light-blue gaze. He faltered and turned aside again and looked as if he were going to fall off the truck.[22]

The action centres on Miss Stokes's determined wooing of the reluctant Joe, and the story gains much of its piquancy and effectiveness from this simple reversal of the conventional sexual roles. The two men are always referred to by their christian names, while Miss Stokes remains Miss Stokes, even to the reader. She has an ironic, detached attitude towards her desire for the boy, of a kind more usually associated with men, and it is clear that he is merely physically attractive to her, no more. 'She glanced him over — save for his slender succulent tenderness she would have despised him.'[23] She therefore places Joe in the unusual position of being a man subjected to explicit sexual attentions which, although unwelcome, he finds difficult to rebuff.

The moral standards of land-girls during the war were a subject of official concern. There exists an entire government file devoted to 'Women's Land Army: Need for More Effective Control', which contains many letters asking for more discipline and a tighter code of conduct, particularly with reference to girls going into public houses, and being out of their billets after 9.30 p.m. In June 1918 a Food Production Department memorandum noted that 'The supply of girls of sufficiently high character to make it safe to send them out to live alone on the farms or in cottages is running short.'[24] Presumably the sexual forwardness of Miss Stokes was the sort of behaviour which incurred official disapproval.

The story develops as a battle between Albert and Miss Stokes for the possession of Joe. At first Albert cannot understand Joe's reluctance to respond to Miss Stokes's overtures; later, when he feels that his friend is being coerced, he fights to win him back into the jokey male comradeship which the arrival of the land-girl had interrupted, and which men have always used as one of the compensations of war. As with the girls in 'Tickets, Please', Miss Stokes's assertiveness is bolstered by her uniform. Albert only manages to break down her composure when he turns up for an appointment in Joe's place, and confronts her as 'a young woman . . . wearing a wide hat of grey straw, and a loose, swinging dress of nigger-grey velvet',[25] instead of her 'linen overalls and gaiters'.[26]

Albert wins the battle, but his victory has a hollow ring. The two men remain uneasy until Miss Stokes leaves the farm. Then 'Joe felt more relieved even than he had felt when he heard the firing cease, after the news had come that the armistice was signed'.[27] The implication is clear — a sexual revolution is more threatening to men than conventional war can ever be.

'The Fox' is also about a land-girl and a soldier, but in this case the soldier, a character very like Joe, takes his revenge on independent women. The models for the main characters were Violet Monk and Cecily Lambert, whom Lawrence met whilst living at Chapel Farm Cottage, Hermitage, Berkshire during 1918. The women, who were cousins, were running nearby Grimsbury Farm. (Even before the war had resulted in women going out to work on the land in large numbers, feminist movements had encouraged agriculture for women as a means to independence; and twelve miles away from Hermitage, at Checkendon, there had been a suffragette dairy and farming school run by two Cambridge graduates, Kate Lelacheur and Fanny Parker, which raised money for the WSPU and trained women in self-sufficiency.)[28] Cecily Lambert has left an account of the ménage at Grimsbury Farm which reveals just how closely much of the circumstantial detail in 'The Fox' was drawn from real life.[29] Violet Monk, like March, was the man about the place, often dressing in men's clothes and doing the rough jobs, while loathing housework; and countless small details of the women's appearance, clothes and mannerisms, the interior of their cottage and so on, find their way into the tale. As usual, though, when using material in this way, Lawrence altered the emotional situation considerably. According to Cecily Lambert, it was Violet Monk, not herself, who was possessive and jealous, and needed looking after; before joining her cousin on the farm Violet had suffered a nervous breakdown. One suspects that Lawrence altered the temperaments of the two women in his portrayal because the story demanded that it be the independent, 'manly' woman who is hunted and tamed. The central plot, Cecily Lambert averred, was 'sheer fantasy'.

'Tickets, Please' shows women uniting to exact surrender from a man. In 'Monkey Nuts' the land-girl, Miss Stokes, intervenes in the relationship between two men, and two struggles ensue: one between Miss Stokes and Joe, for his submission (a struggle in which he is at first overcome but eventually retaliates); the second between Miss Stokes and Albert for possession of Joe. In 'The Fox' this pattern is reversed. It is a young soldier who breaks up an already established relationship between two women, and hunts down not only March, but Banford also, in the battle for the possession and submission of the women he has chosen. At the same time the female solidarity which appears as a potentially positive force in 'Tickets, Please' becomes, in this story, a rather hopeless parasitical relationship between two isolated women. Like 'The Ladybird' and 'The Captain's Doll', which made up the volume in which it appeared, 'The Fox' ends with the prospect of a woman's surrender.

> He did not want her to watch any more, to see any more, to understand any more. He wanted to veil her woman's spirit, as Orientals veil the woman's face. He wanted her to commit herself to him, and to put her independent spirit to sleep. He wanted to take away from her all her effort, all that seemed her very *raison d'être*. He wanted to make her submit, yield, blindly pass away out of all her strenuous consciousness.[30]

Lawrence had described such states before, but as transient moods rather than as permanent states of being. To be fair, 'The Fox' does end on a question mark, like so many of Lawrence's works. We do not *see* March submit in the way that Henry would like her to — she is still struggling against this urging to abdicate all responsibility and thought at the end of the tale, and it would be too simplistic to assume that Lawrence whole-heartedly endorses Henry's attitude. Nevertheless, 'The Fox' and the other two stories that appeared with it imply that the time has come for a new type of relationship to be established between men and women, in which women are to submit to men and relinquish their newly acquired independence. Henry wants March 'not [to] be a man any more, an independent woman with a man's responsibility'.[31] This change is linked directly with the ending of the war. The war is very present in 'The Fox' — the two girls are described as land-girls, although in running the farm themselves rather than working for an employer they are not officially part of the Women's Land Army; there are references to food shortages, daylight saving, and other ways in which the war impinged upon everyday life; and the young man who breaks in upon the women's rural isolation is, of course, a soldier. But it is a war that is more or less over. People are looking to the future, and the life of March and Banford on the farm is seen as a temporary experiment which must end. The possibility of emancipation, the spirit which had inspired the girls in 'Tickets, Please' to take revenge on John Thomas and all that he stands for, and Miss Stokes to seduce her Joe, has been a by-product of war, and things will not be so easy again afterwards.

> 'But what will you do when you've used up all your capital?' he said.
> 'Oh, I don't know,' answered March laconically. 'Hire ourselves out for land-workers, I suppose.'
> 'Yes, but there won't be any demand for women land-workers now the war's over,' said the youth.[32]

The impact of the young man's presence on the isolated life of the two women seems to illustrate the precariousness of their independence. There is a vivid change of perspective from the moment when he first enters their world and laughingly suggests, 'There wants a man about the place.'[33] In all three war stories uniform is a crucial symbol of emancipation for the women, lending them strength and invulnerability. In Henry's presence the men's clothes which March is wearing suddenly seem indecent. 'She was very sensitive in her knees. Having no skirts to cover them, and being forced to sit with them boldly exposed, she suffered.'[34] Yet when she dons 'a dress of dull, green silk crape'[35] the effect is even worse; because of the contrast she feels 'unpeeled and rather exposed . . . almost improper',[36] as if only when wearing men's clothes can she maintain her air of aloof independence.

> She was something quite different. Seeing her always in the hard-cloth breeches, wide on the hips, buttoned on the knee, strong as armour, and in the brown puttees and thick boots, it had never occurred to him that she had a woman's legs and feet. Now it came upon him. She had a woman's soft, skirted legs, and she was accessible. He blushed to the roots of his hair, shoved his nose in his teacup and drank his tea with a little noise that made Banford simply squirm: and, strangely, suddenly he felt a man, no longer a youth. He felt a man, with all a man's grave weight of responsibility. A curious quietness and gravity came over his soul. He felt a man, quiet, with a little of the heaviness of male destiny upon him.
>
> She was soft and accessible in her dress. The thought went home in him like an everlasting responsibility.[37]

March's war-time clothes, it is suggested, have been a suit of armour, making her invulnerable in battle, but they are hardly appropriate everyday wear in peace-time. When she changes out of them she reveals her true, 'womanly' nature: 'she was soft and accessible in her dress'. The story implies that women's assumption of independence and responsibility is as superficial and temporary as their assumption of men's clothes. Henry returns to Bailey Farm believing it still to be his home, and continues to act as though it were, even when the women inform him that they have taken it over. He is cast in the role of the homecoming master, and Banford and March suddenly seem like temporary caretakers — which is indeed exactly the part that women played in relation to men's jobs during the war. The time has come, the story seems to say, for a return to each sex's true role.

'The Fox' foreshadows the concerns that are to appear in Lawrence's work during the twenties. To survey the changes in his attitude in one volume, one cannot do better than look at *The Lost Girl*, a perfect transition-piece clearly spanning Lawrence's pre- and post-war concerns, moving as it does from woman's revolt to woman's submission. It was begun, as *The Insurrection of Miss Houghton*, in 1913, at the same time as *The Sisters* (the first draft of *The Rainbow/Women in Love*). The manuscript was left in Germany during the war, with the story 'three parts done'.[38] Lawrence retrieved it at the beginning of 1920, started it again, and had completed the novel by May of that year.[39]

The main part of the novel, describing Alvina's progressive revolt against the conventions and expectations of provincial life, takes its starting-point very much from the realist tradition. *The Insurrection of Miss Houghton* was partly inspired by Lawrence's reading of Arnold Bennett's *Anna of the Five Towns* (1902) in October 1912. This tightly-controlled realist novel describes the narrow life of a young woman in a strict Wesleyan community in the Potteries, over a short period during which she comes of age, inherits property and its responsibilities, and is engaged to be married. Lawrence was fascinated by the book's Midland setting and its evocation of a community similar to the one in which he had grown up, but he hated what he called Bennett's resignation. He felt that strict realism all too often constituted a pessimistic acceptance of what it described — in this case, the 'oldness and grubbiness and despair'[40] of ordinary English life. It was in connection with Bennett's novel that Lawrence made his famous pronouncement, 'Tragedy ought really to be a great kick at misery.'[41]

The published version of *The Lost Girl* has some noticeable affinities of plot not only with *Anna of the Five Towns* but with the novel that in turn inspired Bennett, George Moore's *A Mummer's Wife* (1885), part of which is also set in the Potteries. This tells the story of a young woman who leaves her invalid husband and his draper's shop to elope with an actor from a variety troupe; after some success as a variety star herself, she is ruined by alcoholism. Christopher Heywood has discussed the relationship of *The Lost Girl* to these two novels,[42] which are part of a realist tradition focusing on the cramped and restricted lives of bourgeois women which may be said to go back to *Madame Bovary* (1857). Lawrence takes the same basic theme of a young woman imprisoned within a constricting routine from which there seems no escape, but Alvina neither submits to convention, as Anna Tellwright does, nor rebels only to suffer worse miseries, like Kate Ede in *A Mummer's Wife*. In fact, Lawrence's determination to portray a successful rebellion (as indicated in the original working title *The Insurrection of Miss Houghton*), would seem to align him also with the writers of the 'problem novel' who dealt rather more specifically with some of the social and economic causes of the heroine's position. There is something about the jaunty tone of *The Lost Girl* which recalls the Wells of *Ann Veronica* (1909), and the very first page of the novel makes reference to Gissing's *The Odd Women* (1893), which Lawrence read in 1910 and which combines realism with the more sociological perspective of the 'problem novel' by introducing characters who are trying to change the conditions that produce their oppression.

> 1913 ... A calm year of plenty. But one chronic and dreary malady: that of the odd women. Why, in the name of all prosperity, should every class but the lowest in such a society hang overburdened with Dead Sea fruit of odd women, unmarried, unmarriageable women, called old maids. Why is it that every tradesman, every schoolmaster, every bank-manager, and every clergyman produces one, two, three or more old maids? Do the middle-classes, particularly the lower middle-classes, give birth to more girls than boys? Or do the lower middle-class men assiduously climb up or down, in marriage, thus leaving their true partners stranded? Or are middle-class women very squeamish in their choice of husbands?
>
> However it be, it is a tragedy. Or perhaps it is not. Perhaps these unmarried women of the middle-classes are the famous sexless Workers of our ant-industrial society, of which we hear so much. Perhaps all they lack is an occupation: in short, a job. – But perhaps we might hear their own opinion, before we lay the law down.[43]

The writing here shows no genuine concern with the socio-economic causes of the so-called 'woman surplus', although in bringing out *The Lost Girl* as 'a perfect selling novel'[44] in 1920 Lawrence may well have been influenced by the fact that the existence of a large proportion of unmarried women, a topical subject in 1913, was even more of a pertinent issue after the war. Women were ejected from their temporary war-work to make room for homecoming soldiers, yet so many men had been wiped out that marriage was a realistic proposition for only a limited number of them. But the passage above shows no clear engagement with the 'problem'. The rambling style, full of 'perhaps's and qualified statements and swift changes of mind, is a sort of empty thinking aloud, frequently used by Lawrence in discussing social questions, which often merely leads to the conclusion that his preoccupations are elsewhere. It represents a kind of parody of the tone adopted by writers like Wells.

Lawrence is interested in the *theme* of a young woman's revolt, but he cares little for either the sociological analysis of the problem novel or the meticulous factual accumulation of realism. Embarking, then, on a novel in the realist mode – a mode which he could, of course, handle more than adequately when he chose – he treats the tradition in which he is writing with scant respect, complaining, for example, that 'it is wearying to repeat the same thing over and over'.⁴⁵ *The Lost Girl* is full of authorial comment undercutting the realist pretensions of the style — 'but why drag it out?', 'now incredible as it may seem', and so on. Faced with the prospect of describing Alvina's period of training as a midwife in London, Lawrence simply gives up — his readers, he says, have heard it all before. 'Surely enough books have been written about heroines in similar circumstances. There is no need to go into the detail of Alvina's six months in Islington.'⁴⁶ He is determined to offer a positive alternative to what he saw as the dreary pessimism of the conventional realist novel.

> Now so far, the story of Alvina is commonplace enough. It is more or less the story of thousands of girls. They all find work. It is the ordinary solution of everything. And if we were dealing with an ordinary girl we should have to carry on mildly and dully down the long years of employment; or, at the best, marriage with some dull school-teacher or office-clerk.
>
> But we protest that Alvina is not ordinary . . . we are not going to follow our song to its fatal and dreary conclusion.⁴⁷

Despite these reservations, *The Lost Girl* may still be regarded in its initial conception as a 'woman-question' novel. This was recognised by the reviewers, for reviews appeared under such titles as 'The Surplus Woman' and 'Frustrate Ladies'.⁴⁸ The pre-war Lawrence was intensely interested in the theme of a young woman breaking out from the conventional life prescribed for her (one should remember that *The Rainbow* was taking shape at around the same time as *The Insurrection of Miss Houghton*), even though he was dissatisfied with the traditional methods of portraying such a rebellion and with its traditional fictional conclusions. Lawrence represents Alvina's revolt as the triumph of a kind of healthy vulgarity over an outdated, false refinement. She escapes from 'the beautiful, but unbearable tyranny' of 'purity and high-mindedness',⁴⁹ as represented by Miss Frost, into the vulgarity of being a midwife, a cinema pianist and a member of a variety troupe. Unlike Kate Ede in *A Mummer's Wife*, her espousal of this kind of life does not lead to tragedy; rather, Alvina's insurrection is essentially a comedy.

The latter part of the novel, dealing with Alvina's marriage to Ciccio, is much more recognisably the work of the post-war Lawrence in its depiction of her submission to a man of another race and another class. For example, the contrast between vulgarity and refinement is replaced by the more radical division between nature and artifice. Alvina's willingness to yield to Ciccio in a passivity tempered by nonchalance and indifference is contrasted with the attitude of Mrs Tuke, an advanced and artistic young woman whom Alvina is attending in childbirth when Ciccio seeks her out for the second time. Mrs Tuke refuses to accept the natural processes that condition her pregnancy, and considers Ciccio's love for Alvina to be just as 'animal' and irrational as her own labour pains. She warns Alvina that what she feels for the Italian is simply atavism — following 'at a man's heel just because he's a man . . . like barbarous women, a slave'.[50] Alvina realises the truth of these accusations — 'I wish he didn't attract me'[51] — but for the first time in her life she is powerless to revolt.

> Why didn't she revolt? Why couldn't she? She was as if bewitched. She couldn't fight against her bewitchment. Why? Because he seemed so beautiful, so beautiful. And this left her numb, submissive. Why must she see him beautiful? Why was she will-less?[52]

Ciccio's power over Alvina does not touch her conscious mind. She is quite capable of seeing him as a common, rather flashy Italian with whom she has virtually nothing in common. 'Her mind remained distinctly clear. She could criticise him, find fault with him, the things he did. But *ultimately*, she could find no fault with him.'[53] We see realised in her the state that Henry had demanded of March in 'The Fox'.

> His love did not stimulate or excite her. It extinguished her. She had to be the quiescent, obscure woman: she felt as if she were veiled . . . Was it atavism, this strange, sleep-like submission to his being? Perhaps it was . . . But it was also heavy and sweet and rich. Somewhere, she was content. Somewhere even she was vastly proud of the dark veiled eternal loneliness she felt, under his shadow . . . a nonchalance deep as sleep, a passivity and indifference so dark and sweet she felt it must be evil.[54]

Only two things temper the novel's exaltation of this trance-like state. The first is that the real hero of the book turns out to be not so much Ciccio as the primitive but breathtakingly beautiful landscape to which he transports her. The writing in the final few chapters set in Italy is of a different order to that in the rest of the book, which increases the reader's conviction that it is the stark but liberating quality of the life encountered by Alvina in Pescocalascio which effects the really radical change in her. 'She had gone beyond the world into the pre-world, she had reopened on the old eternity.'[55] It is in this remote part of Italy that Alvina is finally 'lost — lost — lost utterly',[56] possessed by a 'savage hardness' which issues in terrible despair and wild happiness. The second point which qualifies Alvina's 'atavism' is her feeling that it is a temporary state, something which she must experience for a while but which is not necessarily her final destiny: 'she could never endure it for a life-time. It was only a test on her.'[57] Because of the intricate connection of her state of mind with the Italian landscape, she feels that 'Ciccio must take her to America, or England — to America preferably.'[58]

The last chapter of the novel is called 'Suspense' and the ending is left open, as in so many of Lawrence's novels — Ciccio leaving for the war, Alvina pregnant, the future uncertain; a situation very like that at the end of *Lady Chatterley's Lover*. The distance traversed by Alvina from her upbringing in Woodhouse to her isolation in primitive Italy is immense, and critics have commented on the book's disjointed quality, as if it begins as one novel and ends as another. This can be accounted for not solely by the circumstances of its composition but also by the significant changes that occurred in Lawrence's thinking between the conception of *The Insurrection of Miss Houghton* in 1913 and the final writing of *The Lost Girl* in 1920. It is of course most unlikely that Lawrence ever intended to conclude his heroine's insurrection with, say, a successful career or a conversion to feminism. From the start the emphasis is on the finding of a suitable mate. But the particular form of mating which Lawrence eventually envisages for Alvina, with its insistent emphasis on submission and passivity, is a product of his post-war thinking and his growing anti-feminism.

Notes

1. Vera Brittain, *Testament of Youth* (Victor Gollancz, London, 1933), p. 405.
2. Ruth Adam, *A Woman's Place 1910-1975* (Chatto and Windus, London, 1975), p. 46.
3. Sheila Rowbotham, *Hidden from History* (Pluto Press, London, 1973), p. 110.
4. Quoted in David Mitchell, *Women on the Warpath* (Jonathan Cape, London, 1966), p. 241.
5. Mrs Neville-Rolfe, 'The Changing Moral Standard', *The Nineteenth Century and After*, vol. 84 (1918), p. 725.
6. Neil Myers, 'Lawrence and the War', *Criticism*, vol. 4, no. 1 (1962), p. 44.

7. Ibid., p. 45.
8. Letter to Gordon Campbell, 21 September 1914, *Letters*, vol. 2, p. 218.
9. Letter to Lady Cynthia Asquith, 21 October 1915. Ibid., p. 415.
10. Letter to Lady Cynthia Asquith, 2 November 1915. Ibid., p. 425.
11. Letter to Hugh Meredith, 2 November 1915. Ibid., p. 426.
12. Letter to Katherine Mansfield, 21 November 1918. *Collected Letters*, p. 565.
13. 'Tickets, Please' and 'The Fox' were written in November 1918, at almost exactly the same time as the letter to Katherine Mansfield; 'Monkey Nuts' was written in May 1919. See Keith Sagar, *D.H. Lawrence: A Calendar of his Works* (Manchester University Press, Manchester, 1979), pp. 90 and 94.
14. Unpublished letter to Robert Mountsier, 20 January 1917 (Humanities Research Center, The University of Texas at Austin).
15. Letter to Edward Garnett, 22 April 1914. *Letters*, vol. 2, p. 165.
16. Lionel Trilling, *Prefaces to the Experience of Literature* (Oxford University Press, Oxford, 1981), p. 124.
17. *England, My England*, p. 42.
18. Ibid., p. 43.
19. Ibid., p. 48.
20. Ibid., p. 51.
21. The myth of the death of Pentheus at the hands of the Bacchantes has been suggested as a possible source for the story; see George H. Ford, *Double Measure* (Holt, Rinehart and Winston, New York, 1965), p. 94. It has also been conjectured that Lawrence may have been drawing on his own experience as a youth at the hands of the women workers in the surgical goods factory where he was briefly employed; they are said to have humiliated him by cornering him and forcibly exposing his genitals. See Harry T. Moore, *The Priest of Love* (revised edition, Heinemann, London, 1974), p. 43.
22. *England, My England*, pp. 77-8.
23. Ibid., p. 80.
24. Arthur Marwick, *Women at War 1914-1918* (Fontana, London, 1977), p. 101.
25. *England, My England*, p. 87.
26. Ibid., p. 77.
27. Ibid., p. 90.
28. Antonia Raeburn, *The Militant Suffragettes* (Michael Joseph, London, 1973), pp. 142-3, and *Spare Rib*, August 1977, p. 13.
29. Edward Nehls (ed.), *D.H. Lawrence: A Composite Biography* (3 vols., University of Wisconsin Press, Madison, 1957-9), vol. 1, pp. 463-7.
30. *Three Novellas*, p. 157.
31. Ibid., p. 158.
32. Ibid., pp. 96-7.
33. Ibid., p. 97.
34. Ibid., p. 95.
35. Ibid., p. 132.
36. Ibid., p. 134.
37. Ibid., p. 133.
38. Letter to Martin Secker, 27 December 1919. *Collected Letters*, p. 602.
39. Sagar, *D.H. Lawrence: A Calendar of his Works*, pp. 99-101.
40. Letter to Arthur McLeod, 4 October 1912. *Letters*, vol. 1, p. 459.
41. Ibid.
42. Christopher Heywood, 'D.H. Lawrence's *The Lost Girl* and its Antecedents by George Moore and Arnold Bennett', *English Studies*, vol. 47, no. 2 (1966), pp. 131-4. Another possible antecedent for Lawrence's novel is E.M. Forster's *Where Angels Fear to Tread* (1905), in which an English widow marries an Italian inferior to her in social status and many years her junior. The contrast

between English suburban existence and the romantic yet vulgar life of an Italian hill town is central to both novels, as is the attraction which the Latin male holds for Englishwomen.

43. *The Lost Girl*, pp. 1-2.
44. Letter to Martin Secker, 27 December 1919. *Collected Letters*, p. 602.
45. *The Lost Girl*, p. 18.
46. Ibid., p. 32.
47. Ibid., pp. 83 and 85.
48. Francis Hackett, 'The Surplus Woman', *New Republic*, 16 March 1921, pp. 77-8; 'Frustrate Ladies' (unsigned), *Nation* (New York), 7 September 1921, p. 269.
49. *The Lost Girl*, p. 36.
50. Ibid., p. 286.
51. Ibid., p. 283.
52. Ibid., p. 288.
53. Ibid.
54. Ibid.
55. Ibid., p. 316.
56. Ibid., p. 313.
57. Ibid., p. 320.
58. Ibid.

4 THE CONTEXT OF LAWRENCE'S SEXUAL THEORY

Lawrence's shifting attitude to the relationship between the sexes is graphically illustrated by the changes that occur in his theories about sex. When he wrote of England in 1913 that 'only through a readjustment between men and women, and a making free and healthy of the sex, will she get out of her present atrophy',[1] he was representative of the progressive thought of his age. During the Edwardian years the discussion of sex had to some extent opened up, at least among intellectuals and 'advanced' people, and a new subject, 'sex-psychology', made its appearance. It remained predominantly an amateur's field, and the most significant contributions to it were made not by practising scientists but by men of letters. The two great pioneers and populariser of sex-psychology in England were Havelock Ellis and Edward Carpenter.[2] Both combined a strong desire to free society from the oppressiveness of Victorian prudery and ignorance with a genuine curiosity about the nature of human sexuality, and a wide-ranging interest in literature, philosophy, politics, anthropology, psychology, mysticism and the occult; and both were champions of a large number of radical causes, including the women's movement.

Of course, sexual liberation in itself is by no means synonymous with the lifting of women's oppression, but it would seem that the overall influence of sex-psychology at the turn of the century was for the benefit of women. It is at first surprising, then, to realise that sexual liberation hardly figured at all in the programme of the organised feminist movement, and scarcely seems to have been discussed in a feminist context, except by isolated individuals (as it always has been) and in controversial organs like the *Freewoman*, which was in dissent from mainstream feminism and was criticised for 'wallowing in sex-consciousness'.[3] The double standard of morality was certainly discussed in, for example, the suffrage organisations, but the tendency was to argue that the low moral standards of men should be raised to correspond to the high standards expected of women; in 1913 the WSPU adopted the slogan 'Votes for Women and Purity for Men'. Discussion of female sexuality was still largely taboo, and to many feminists sexual freedom meant simply an increase in the twin evils of venereal disease and prostitution. In addition there were some women's organisations such as the Women's League which were specifically committed to raising the moral tone of the nation. The relation between feminism and sex-psychology was thus complex, and at times one-sided.[4] The same is true of the relationship between feminism and the birth-control movement, which was also growing rapidly at this time. The controversy over contraception and 'the race' was in fact a crucial focus for the discussion of sexuality; the nature of the debate can be summed up as pleasure versus procreation. The 'establishment' view was that sexuality existed purely for the procreation of children inside the institution of marriage, and that only the fear of illegitimate pregnancy kept young girls from vice. A typical comment was that contraception would 'degrade the finer moral instincts of both men and women, especially, of course, the latter: in them it cannot have any other effect than to bring about a bestial sensuality and indifference to all morality'.[5] On the other hand, an important strand in the argument of the radical champions of birth-control was that sexuality existed primarily for personal satisfaction and pleasure and as an expression of love, and need not necessarily result in the procreation of children except when this was desired. Again, there was no feminist consensus on this matter: some feminists were in favour of contraception because of the control that it offered to women over their own bodies; others believed in abstinence and 'spiritual' relationships between enlightened men and women; still others saw in contraception an excuse for men to indulge their sexual appetites without the responsibility of commitment or paternity, and feared that women would be exploited rather than helped by it.

Lawrence's early non-fictional writing on sexual theory, mainly to be found in the *Study of Thomas Hardy* (written in 1914 but not published during his lifetime), is thus to be seen against this background of a growing interest in sex-psychology and an intense public debate on sexual morality. Knowledge of Freud's work came late to England, and at the time of Lawrence's early writings the subject was still dominated by the gentlemen-scholars Ellis and Carpenter. Also influential were the writings of two German philosophers — Schopenhauer's *On Women* and *The Metaphysics of Love*, and *Sex and Character* by Otto Weininger.[6] These two writers are now notorious for their misogyny, but Weininger's theories were used — selectively — by Ellis and Carpenter and by feminists themselves.[7]

Sex-psychology was, then, very much in the air at the time when Lawrence was writing the *Study of Thomas Hardy*. How much he specifically drew on the work of the sex-psychologists is more difficult to determine. He certainly read Schopenhauer's essays while still a student and annotated *The Metaphysics of Love*.[8] The case for his knowledge of Carpenter's work is exhaustively set out in Emile Delavenay's *D.H. Lawrence and Edward Carpenter*, and it seems probable that he had read at least some of Carpenter's works on sexuality by 1914. The argument for Lawrence's acquaintance with Weininger's book is less certain, and rests to a large extent on the assumption that he was introduced to it by Philip Heseltine in Cornwall during 1916. (Heseltine had been interested in sex-psychology at Oxford and 'had read Havelock Ellis, Carpenter and Otto Weininger'.)[9] However, the first meeting between Lawrence and Heseltine took place a year after the writing of the Hardy study, and unfortunately Delavenay's claim that the study shows signs of Weininger's influence is based solely on internal textual evidence; but it is certainly possible that Lawrence had read *Sex and Character* before 1914, maybe in Germany. Similarly, there is no direct evidence that Lawrence knew of Havelock Ellis's work at this stage, although some of Ellis's prolific journalistic output, if not one of his books, is almost certain to have reached him at some point.[10]

However, the justification for looking at the sexual theory of the Hardy study against the background of sex-psychology is not to detect specific sources and influences in Lawrence's work, but to point to a pool of common notions and theories available for the discussion of sexuality at this time. There were intrinsic similarities in the writings of both pro- and anti-feminist authors, and Lawrence, in 1914 at least, may be precariously grouped with the former. Carpenter and Ellis, who were sympathetic allies of feminism, rely to a large extent on the same theories and categories as the misogynist Weininger; their differing ideological stances depend on the different values they assign to the same concepts.

That Lawrence's most important discussion of sex-psychology should appear in a work ostensibly about the novels of Hardy is in itself an interesting point. Hardy was of course attacked for his frank treatment of sexuality, particularly in *Tess of the d'Urbervilles* (1891) and *Jude the Obscure* (1895). Critics saw the latter novel as propaganda for 'free love',[11] and one complained that it was not a novel at all but 'a treatise on sexual pathology'.[12] Radicals, on the other hand, tended to be admirers of Hardy when this was still unfashionable: Havelock Ellis, for example, published a lucid defence of *Jude the Obscure* in the *Savoy* in 1896.[13] Hardy's novels were therefore used during this period as a focus for the discussion of sexuality; and Lawrence's study, though idiosyncratic, is not as far outside the tradition of radical debate on sexuality as it may seem at first sight.

Crucial to the Hardy study is a sense of the immense significance of sexuality and sexual difference. On a personal level, Lawrence proclaims that 'the turning pivot of a man's life is his sex-life, the centre and swivel of his being is the sexual act'.[14] But sex is more than a matter of personal fulfilment. For Lawrence, the source of all life was in 'the great male and female duality and unity'.[15] All the writers under discussion agree on the supreme, cosmic importance of the division into sexes. Carpenter writes:

> Sex is the allegory of Love in the physical world. It is from this fact that it derives its immense power . . . whoever has truly found another has found not only that other, and with that other himself, but has found also a third — who dwells at the centre and holds the plastic material of the universe in the palm of his hand, and is a creator of sensible forms.[16]

Such lofty claims had been made during the Victorian period for *love*, but never for *sex*. In *Sex and Character* Weininger writes: 'the problem of woman and of woman's rights . . . is bound intimately with the deepest riddles of existence. It can be solved, practically or theoretically, morally or metaphysically, only in relation to an interpretation of the cosmos.'[17] This conviction that sex was to be taken very seriously indeed was one reason why there was not as much feminist opposition to Weininger as might have been expected; an article on Weininger in the *Freewoman* in 1912 put the view that 'a false philosophy of sex is more complimentary to woman than the wish-wash of sentiment and condescension that usurps its place in this country'.[18] A glimpse of the seemingly infinite nature of the sexual split often resulted in a sceptical attitude towards the mere patching-up of the social fabric which was seen to be the goal of 'women's rights' reformers. Lawrence and Weininger, in particular, shared the feeling that such a cosmic riddle could not be solved by piecemeal changes in law and habits. Even Carpenter and Ellis, despite the support that each gave to a large number of reforms, were in this respect essentially revolutionaries.

One of the most significant themes of Lawrence's sexual theory in the *Study of Thomas Hardy* is that sexual pleasure and self-realisation are more important than the reproductive process. The study opens with the image of the poppy, whose scarlet flower serves no utilitarian purpose but is formed from that 'excess' which is really 'the thing itself at its maximum of being'.[19] On this transient, wasteful but significant flower, Lawrence builds his ethic of self-realisation. 'Not the fruit . . . but the flower is the culmination and climax, the degree to be striven for.'[20] This general principle is particularly relevant to sexuality, for through sexuality the most basic act of self-preservation, the creation of a new generation, is achieved; yet, for Lawrence, sexuality is also 'the *via media* to being, for man or woman'.[21] He had already explored this paradox in the poem 'Rose of All the World', where he muses on the fact that the sexual act, whose utilitarian function is the creation of new life, is also the means to self-discovery — another kind of 'new life' — in the participants. Disputing the traditional view that 'the seed is purpose, blossom accident', he concludes

> To me it seems the seed is just left over
> From the red rose-flowers' fiery transience.[22]

Corresponding to the 'useless' scarlet flower of the poppy is the 'functionless' female orgasm, which has no utilitarian part to play in reproduction, but is pure pleasure.

The idea that reproduction is simply a by-product of the far more significant process of achieving one's individuality is fully explored in Chapter 6 of the *Study of Thomas Hardy* ('The Axle and the Wheel of Eternity'). It is a radical view in that it relegates woman's role as childbearer to a minor position and asks her to join the same quest for selfhood as man.

> That she bear children is not a woman's significance. But that she bear herself, that is her supreme and risky fate: that she drive on to the edge of the unknown, and beyond. She may leave children behind, for security. It is arranged so.
>
> It is so arranged that the very act which carries us out into the unknown shall probably deposit seed for security to be left behind. But the act, called the sexual act, is not for the depositing of the seed. It is for leaping off into the unknown, as from a cliff's edge, like Sappho into the sea.[23]

Carpenter's position on this question is very close to Lawrence's and it is likely that he was one of Lawrence's major inspirations. Carpenter originally developed his thesis as part of his argument for the recognition and acceptance of homosexuality, which was commonly considered unnatural or perverse because it was non-reproductive.

> Regeneration is the key to the meaning of love — to be in the first place born again *in* some one else or *through* some one else; in the second place only, to be born again through a child . . . generation alone can hardly be looked upon as the primary object of conjugation.[24]

Havelock Ellis saw the importance of this concept for feminism and linked it in more practical fashion to the need for contraception and the recognition of female sexuality. His views are expressed in the many articles he wrote on the subject for popular, scientific and radical journals.[25]

Another of the more controversial concepts that Lawrence explores in the Hardy study is that male and female are only relative terms, and that each individual is a complex mixture, both physically and psychologically, of male and female elements. 'Every man comprises male and female in his being, the male always struggling for predominance. A woman likewise consists in male and female, with female predominant.'[26] Androgyny had of course been a predominant theme in the decadent literature of the nineteenth century and in the occult writings of all ages, but the use of the concept had been primarily symbolic.[27] Intrinsic bisexuality as a scientific theory with important psychological implications does not seem to have been in common circulation before the 1900s. Weininger appears to have been the originator and populariser of the theory, and some indication of the importance that was attached to it can be gained from the fact that Wilhelm Fliess, a colleague of Freud, complained that Weininger had stolen the idea from him and beaten him in publishing what Fliess obviously regarded as a vital piece of work.[28] Weininger elaborated a complex world-view on the idea of a 'permanent bisexual condition'.[29] Not surprisingly, he had a sympathetic attitude towards homosexuality, and his ideas were taken up and popularised by Carpenter in his vindication of the 'intermediate sex'.

> It is beginning to be recognised that the sexes do not or should not normally form two groups hopelessly isolated in habit and feeling from each other, but that they rather represent the two poles of *one* group — which is the human race; so that while certainly the extreme specimens at either pole are vastly divergent, there are great numbers in the middle region who (though differing corporeally as

men and women) are by emotion and temperament very near to each other.[30]

This concept was an important one for feminism. It questioned the idea that everyone should conform to a 'manly' or 'womanly' stereotype and allowed women to come to terms with 'unwomanly' aspects of their personalities. Florence Farr, a 'New Woman' very much in the public eye, wrote that it was 'very difficult to classify temperaments without alluding to Weininger's *Sex and Character*', and praised 'the ingenious theory that virile men and feminine women are the rarest creatures on earth, and that the great majority of us are made up of various proportions of the two sexes'.[31] Many other women must have found this a useful and liberating notion. We know, for example, that Helen Corke found Carpenter's work on the subject encouraging and helpful when she was struggling with what she thought was a deficiency in her femininity.[32]

Weininger evolved a law of sexual attraction from this theory of the mixture of male and female in each person. This postulated 'a maximum degree of sexual attraction between individuals, one of which possesses just as much femaleness as the other possesses maleness',[33] so that their union would bring together the ingredients for one 'perfect male' and one 'perfect female'. This is similar to Lawrence's idea in the *Study of Thomas Hardy* that sexual love involves the exchange of maleness and femaleness between the partners, so that the man becomes 'pure male' and the woman 'pure female'.

> In Love, in the act of love, that which is mixed in me becomes pure, that which is female in me is given to the female, that which is male in her draws into me, I am complete, I am pure male, she is pure female.[34]

Sexual love is thus a process in which one's sexual identity is defined and asserted by transferring to one's partner those elements in oneself which belong to the opposite sex. Also implicit in Lawrence's formulation is the idea of the interchange of vital essences during sexual contact, a prevalent notion which Schopenhauer also described, and which Carpenter thought important.

At the centre of the Hardy study is an elaborate schema of sexual dualism. Lawrence, rejecting such traditional philosophical dichotomies as body and mind or appearance and reality, extends sexual differentiation into a cosmic principle. 'It may be said that male and female are terms relative only to physical sex. But this is the consistent indication of the greater meaning.'[35] For Lawrence everything is sexed; it is *the* fundamental division. The Hardy study is permeated with a sense of sex-designated opposites. Maleness comprises Knowledge, the Spirit, Motion, Love, the Hub, Doing, Separateness, Consciousness, Individuality, Timelessness, Thought and the religion of the Son; Femaleness is Nature, the Flesh, Stability, Law, the Axle, Being, Monism, Unconsciousness, Oneness, the Moment, Feeling, and the religion of the Father. There are some surprises; the classification of the Old Testament spirit, the law of the Father, as female, and the New Testament spirit, the love of the Son, as male, is a curious distinction and seems to be original to Lawrence; although in the view of the anti-semite and anti-feminist Weininger, Jewishness and femaleness had much in common. Yet in general Lawrence's divisions are predictable. Man is transcendent, individual, active *mind*; woman immanent, undifferentiated, passive *matter*. 'The male exists in doing, the female in being.'[36] And what the sexes have to offer each other can be stated as follows: 'In woman man finds his root and establishment. In man woman finds her exfoliation and florescence.'[37] It will be seen, however, that, at the time of writing the *Study of Thomas Hardy*, Lawrence was not on the side of one set of qualities as opposed to the other. He endorses feeling, for example (a 'female' principle), but also individuality (a 'male' principle). There is not, as in Weininger, a denunciation of all the so-called female qualities.

Such schemes of sexual dualism were common mental property for the discussion of sexuality and the 'woman question'. In Weininger the terminology is extreme, but essentially the same. 'Mankind occurs as male or female, as something or nothing . . . The relation of man to woman is simply that of subject to object.'[38] Some other categories used by Weininger are the familiar ones of Reason/Emotion, Consciousness/Unconsciousness, Activity/Passivity, Form/Matter, Morality/Amorality and Intelligence/Sexuality. His difference from Lawrence is made clear when he says that 'genius declares itself to be a kind of higher masculinity . . . identical with the highest and widest consciousness'.[39] Lawrence abhors those geniuses whom he considers exclusively 'male', such as Goethe and Shelley ('I can think of no being in the world so transcendently male as Shelley . . . he did not belong to life')[40] and, in the Hardy study at least, is concerned with the right balance between the two poles of male and female.

Havelock Ellis's *Man and Woman*, a more scientific study, had reached very similar conclusions about the nature of the difference between the sexes. For Ellis, man was biologically more variable, approached more to the senile type, and was more rational than woman. She, on the other hand, was biologically the more stable sex, approached more to the infantile type, and was more emotional. Ellis talks of the 'affectability' of women, their 'greater emotionality' and the strength of their 'more primitive nervous centres'.[41] Like Lawrence, he concluded that 'this organically primitive nature of women, in form and function and instinct, is always restful to men tortured by their vagrant energies'.[42] He agreed with Weininger that 'the artistic impulse is vastly more spontaneous, more pronounced, and more widely spread among men than among women',[43] but argued that this was because genius was a pathological condition which was less likely to occur in women, as they kept closer to the norm. There are no value-judgements in Ellis's account, which is basically an anthology of the scientific and semi-scientific work that had been done on the subject to date. But we know that Ellis looked forward to a future in which the 'female' side of life would predominate. He hinted that 'organic conservatism may often involve political revolution',[44] and thought that the liberation of women would bring 'a reinvigoration as complete as any brought by barbarians to an effete and degenerating civilization'.[45]

Carpenter too accepted the traditional divisions. For him, man was active, energetic, hungry, productive, wandering, rational, cosmic in scope; woman passive, quiescent, assimilative, reproductive, stable, emotional; narrower, yet closer to 'the great unconscious processes of Nature'.[46] He, too, saw man as the restless traveller returning to woman for rest and stability.

> It is to her that Man, after his excursions and wanderings, mental and physical, continually tends to return as to his primitive home and resting-place, to restore his balance, to find his centre of life, and to draw stores of energy and inspiration for fresh conquests of the outer world.[47]

While recognising the part played by social conditioning in producing differences between the sexes, Carpenter continued to believe in a split along the traditional lines that was more or less ineradicable.

> It is commonly received opinion that woman tends more to intuition and man to logic; and certainly the male mind seems better able to deal with abstractions and generalisations, and the female mind with the personal and the detailed and the concrete. And while

the difference may be in part attributable to the artificial confinement of women to the domestic sphere, there is probably something more organic in it than that . . . Generally it will be admitted, as we are dealing with points of mental and moral difference between the sexes, Man has developed the more active, and Woman the more passive qualities; and it is pretty obvious, here too, that this difference is not only due to centuries of inequality and of property marriage, but roots back in some degree to the very nature of their respective sexual functions.[48]

Yet Carpenter, like Ellis, saw nothing oppressive to women in calling them passive, emotional, stable and so on; both writers believed that society had become too technological and industrial, too logical and commercial, in short too masculine, and put much of their faith for the future in the possibilities of feminist revolution and the 'feminising' of many areas of life.

The idea of history as a cycle of masculine and feminine eras is of course to be found in the *Study of Thomas Hardy*, where it forms the basis of Lawrence's historical and aesthetic analysis. To some extent in the Hardy study (but at more length in *Twilight in Italy*, written in 1912-13, revised in 1915, and therefore very much of the same period as the Hardy study) Lawrence also plots these male and female cycles in different races. Such concepts were widespread. Weininger had seen the present age as too feminised and wanted a resurgence of male logical power; he had also classified races according to their maleness or femaleness, with Aryans as the most male and Jews as the most female.

It will be seen from this summary that Lawrence's sexual theory in the *Study of Thomas Hardy* belongs with the writings of the sex-psychologists, and that there existed a common pool of concepts of masculinity and femininity which were used by all the writers concerned. The facts are more or less taken for granted, but are interpreted differently according to the personal outlook of the author. Thus, for both Lawrence and Weininger woman represents the 'unknown', 'unconsciousness', 'earthiness'. For Lawrence this is a challenge and a source of joy. He talks of 'the gladness of a man in contact with the unknown in the female . . . the advancing into the unknown . . . the landing on the shore of the undiscovered half of the world, where the wealth of the female lies before us'.[49] For Weininger the female qualities are a terrifying threat to the supremacy of male logic and rationality, and he speaks of 'the deepest fear of man; the fear of the woman, which is the fear of unconsciousness, the alluring abyss of annihilation'.[50] Lawrence, however, is not presenting a case in the same way as Carpenter or Ellis. The Hardy study is not explicitly polemical, like some of his later theorising on sexuality. It is a piece of imaginative writing distinguished from the work of the sex-psychologists by its poetic language. The prose of Ellis and Carpenter is measured, cool and down-to-earth, designed to persuade, convince or inform, rather than to please; and both seem to have found an effective style for the discussion of previously unmentionable subjects. Weininger's work is couched in the terminology of German transcendentalist philosophy and charged with hysteria. But the *Study of Thomas Hardy* belongs to the period of *The Rainbow* with its beautiful rhythmic prose, and is full of some of Lawrence's best writing. What he advocates in the Hardy study is a sensitive openness and receptiveness between men and women, saying that we must accept the challenge of sexual difference and use sexuality as a means of 'plunging into the unknown', rather than for the taking of selfish pleasure. And the final emphasis is on balance or relatedness, the feeling that each sex is necessary to the other.

In 1914, then, Lawrence is essentially writing in the same spirit as the sex-psychologists; and that spirit is, taken as a whole, sympathetic to feminism, despite its adherence to rigid sexual categories. Lawrence's post-war writings on sexuality demonstrate how radically his sympathies changed towards the end of the war. His later work on sexual theory is more diffuse, but a representative statement can be found in *Fantasia of the Unconscious* (1923). This is characterised by a sexual determinism which is quite different from the flexibility and emphasis on relationship which are found in the Hardy study.

Like its predecessor, *Psychoanalysis and the Unconscious, Fantasia of the Unconscious* is ostensibly a refutation of Freudianism. Lawrence's acquaintance with Freud's work was secondhand, derived firstly from Frieda and her sister Else's circle in Germany, and secondly from some English Freudians whom he came to know, notably David Eder and Barbara Low.[51] Frieda wrote, 'I don't remember whether he had read Freud or heard of him before we met in 1912. But I was a great Freud admirer; we had long arguments.'[52] However, the spirit of 'Freudianism' which Frieda had encountered was a libertarian creed of sexual freedom. 'I believed that if only sex were "free" the world would straightaway turn into a paradise.'[53] As Frederick Hoffman has remarked, 'most people who read Freud ... but did not study him carefully thought that he was an advocate of free love who argued that sexual freedom was the only pathway to happiness'.[54]

The German face of sex-psychology which Frieda knew is of interest because it combined sexual liberation with a kind of matriarchal feminism in a fashion virtually unknown in England. One of the principal spokesmen for this 'erotic movement' was the charismatic Otto Gross, with whom both Frieda and Else had affairs. The full impact of the movement on Lawrence is discussed by Martin Green in his book on the Von Richthofen sisters. According to Green, 'matriarchal rebellion was one of the most sharply characterised forms of the erotic movement',[55] which stood for 'life-values, for eroticism, for the value of myth and primitive cultures, for the superiority of instinct and intuition to the values of science, for the primacy of the female mode of being'.[56] It was more likely to have been Gross's ideas on free love, rather than anything strictly derived from Freud's writings, that Frieda conveyed to Lawrence in the first years of their relationship. Some of Lawrence's early letters to her show that he was temporarily influenced by the gospel of sexual freedom — in one, he tells her to take other lovers in his absence if she wishes to.[57] Sympathy with the tenets of the German 'erotic movement', with its idealisation of female sexuality and maternity, is evident in the stress on sexual love as the highest form of human activity in the Hardy study and in the portrayal of the matriarchal women of the first part of *The Rainbow*, confident in their motherhood and sexually active. Indeed, as critics have pointed out, *The Rainbow* is a matriarchal work, dominated by the image of the womb, and its celebrations of sexuality and fertility are conducted not in terms of phallic power, but of the rhythmic cycles of gestation and birth.

In Lawrence's post-war bitterness it is first of all against this concept of woman as earth-mother, life-giver and high-priestess that he revolts. He had already shown Birkin reacting against the 'Magna Mater' in *Women in Love*. A clearer indication of a change in his thought can be seen in the crucial letter written to Katherine Mansfield at the very end of the war, in November 1918. Lawrence is sending Katherine and Middleton Murry a book by Jung: probably *The Psychology of the Unconscious*, which had been published in English in 1916. It is a psychological study of myths and symbols, and although Lawrence objected to its heavy reliance on the concept of the Oedipus complex ('this mother-incest idea can become an obsession'), he drew from the book — and especially, one imagines, from the chapter entitled 'The Battle for Deliverance from the Mother' — his own moral.

> But it seems to me there is this much truth in it: that at certain periods the man has a desire and a tendency to return into the woman, make her his goal and end, find his justification in her. In this way he casts himself as it were into her womb, and she, the Magna Mater, receives him with gratification . . . It is awfully hard, once the sex relation has gone this way, to recover. If we don't recover, we die.[58]

Lawrence now sees his pre-war emphasis on the sexual relationship as a concession to the dominating maternal female. The letter is the first direct expression of a belief in male superiority, whose possible historical origins I have attempted to trace in the preceding chapter. Already, in 1916, Lawrence had written to Cynthia Asquith that 'love' was no longer a solution to anything: 'the old order is done for, toppling on top of us: . . . it's no use the men looking to the women for salvation, nor the women looking to sensuous satisfaction for their fulfilment'.[59] At the time of the letter to Katherine Mansfield in 1918, he had just completed the essay 'Education of the People', which resembles *Fantasia of the Unconscious* in tone and contains many similar ideas. It is a violent, often sadistic attack on democracy and liberal idealism, in the ranting style that now begins to characterise Lawrence's writing. Much of this vitriolic anger is directed against maternity.

> Babies should invariably be taken away from their modern mothers and given, not to yearning and maternal old maids, but to rather stupid fat women who can't be bothered with them. There should be a league for the prevention of maternal love, as there is a society for the prevention of cruelty to animals. The stupid fat woman may not guard so zealously against germs. But all the germs in the list of bacteriology are not so dangerous for a child as mother-love.[60]

The reaction against maternity is part of a larger reaction against the feminine values of love and emotion, although Lawrence was to restore these to their former favoured position in his scale of values after he had re-labelled them 'masculine'. He is now concerned to establish a sexual hierarchy in place of his former emphasis on balance and relatedness. One sex is to be given priority over the other.

> Action and utterance, which are male, are polarized against feeling, emotion, which are female. And which is positive, which negative?

> Was man, the eternal protagonist, born of woman, from her womb of fathomless emotion? Or was woman, with her deep womb of emotion, born from the rib of active man, the first created? Man, the doer, the knower, the original in *being*, is he lord of life? Or is woman, the great Mother, who bore us from the womb of love, is she the supreme Goddess?
>
> This is the question of all time. And as long as man and woman endure, so will the answer be given, first one way, then the other.[61]

This question is at the real core of *Fantasia of the Unconscious*. Lawrence of course realised that the answer to it would be historically determined; just as Matthew Arnold in *Culture and Anarchy* had acknowledged that there would be times when society needed 'Hebraising' as well as times when it needed 'Hellenising', so Lawrence asserts that there are periods when 'femininisation' is needed, and periods when masculine values must predominate.

If we compare some of the notions about sexuality which appear in *Fantasia of the Unconscious* with those which Lawrence had expressed in the Hardy study, crucial differences appear. Sexuality, which had taken pride of place in the Hardy study as the highest form of human activity and human expression, is now relegated to a secondary position. A greater impulse than the sexual is 'the desire of the human male to build a world', 'the pure disinterested craving of the human male to make something wonderful, out of his own head and his own self, and his own soul's faith and delight'.[62] This is an important part of Lawrence's case against Freud — a case which is in many respects the same as that of the establishment of the time, namely that it is obsessive and unhealthy to attribute a sexual motive to all human activity. Lawrence's reaction to psychoanalysis is that of a person who sees his own ideas on the crucial nature of sexual experience taken further than he would like, and in a different direction. The reaction against sexuality and the reaction against femininity are inextricably bound up. Lawrence's abrupt association of sexuality with women ('the sex') is a step backwards to a Victorian position. The problem of the place and importance of sexuality is temporarily shelved by assigning it, along with emotion, love, sympathy and so on, exclusively to women; and then saying that men — and only men — must achieve the correct balance between the 'male' and 'female' worlds.

Of course there should be a great balance between the sexes. Man, in the daytime, must follow his own soul's greatest impulse, and give himself to life-work and risk himself to death. It is not woman who claims the highest in man . . . the woman has her world, her positivity: the world of love, of emotion, of sympathy. And it behoves every man in his hour to take off his shoes and relax and give himself up to his woman and her world.[63]

In this facile assigning of stereotyped roles we have not progressed beyond the Victorian notion of the separate spheres. Work, or some collective purpose, is the highest virtue, and it is exclusively male; love is important, but secondary, and female. Man may move between the two spheres, or at least retire to the second one now and again for rest and comfort, but woman is consigned for ever to her domestic, twilit world of the emotions. Sexuality is no longer a symbol of the union of opposites. In Lawrence's dialectic it has itself become a term in the argument, to be pitched against its own opposite, purposive (male) activity.

Assert sex as the predominant fulfilment, and you get the collapse of living purpose in man. You get anarchy. Assert *purposiveness* as the one supreme and pure activity of life, and you drift into barren sterility, like our business life of today, and our political life.[64]

Lawrence starts to run into logical difficulties in his new assertion of male collective activity as the highest good, since that kind of activity is too easily associated with the 'sterility' of industrialism and capitalism, our 'business and political life'. Indeed, he continues to stand up for instinct against reason, intuition against science, sensuality against spirituality — in other words, for those values traditionally considered female. His solution is to take over those values and re-name them masculine — and to achieve this, he attributes the worst excesses of modern self-consciousness and idealism to (perverted) women.

Accompanying this revolt against the domination of the sexual relationship and what Lawrence saw as 'female' modes of being is a return to the concept of a rigid dichotomy between the sexes. In the Hardy study Lawrence had put forward the relatively radical idea of a shifting spectrum of bisexuality in each individual, but now he drives home the notion of a great gulf between the sexes by a continual thudding emphasis on the words 'male' and 'female'.

A child is born sexed. A child is either male or female; the whole of its psyche and physique is either male or female. Every single living cell is either male or female, and will remain either male or female as long as life lasts. And every single cell in every male child is male, and every cell in every female child is female. The talk about a third sex, or about the indeterminate sex, is just to pervert the issue.[65]

Lawrence now talks of the 'hermaphrodite fallacy',[66] arguing that 'the gulf between . . . the most womanly man on earth, and the most manly woman, is just the same as ever'.[67] If the two sexes appear to share a large proportion of attributes, or if characteristics traditionally associated with one sex appear in the other, this can only be a result of the reversal of the true roles.

Man, in the midst of all his effeminacy, is still male and nothing but male. And woman, though she harangue in Parliament or patrol the streets with a helmet on her head, is still completely female. They are only playing each other's roles, because the poles have swung into reversion. The compass is reversed. But that doesn't mean that the north pole has become the south pole, or that each is a bit of both.[68]

These are all radical changes, and illustrate the complete volte-face that occurred in Lawrence's thinking at the end of the war. He was not alone in his convictions, as I suggest in the next chapter. But he had departed for ever from the tradition of liberal sex-psychology, broadly sympathetic to feminist ideals, with which his earlier theoretical work had had much in common.

Notes

1. Letter to Arthur McLeod, 23 April 1913. *Letters*, vol. 1, p. 544.
2. See Sheila Rowbotham and Jeffrey Weeks, *Socialism and the New Life* (Pluto Press, London, 1977) and Paul Robinson, *The Modernization of Sex* (Paul Elek, London, 1976), Ch. 1.
3. Letter to the editors, *Freewoman*, 7 December 1911, p. 56.
4. See Constance Rover, *Love, Morals and the Feminists* (Routledge and Kegan Paul, London, 1970).
5. R. Ussher, *Neo-Malthusianism* (Gibbings, London, 1898), p. 78. See J.A. and Olive Banks, *Feminism and Family Planning in Victorian England* (Liverpool University Press, Liverpool, 1964).
6. *Sex and Character* was published in English in 1906. Weininger had committed suicide in 1903 at the age of 23, two years after the publication of his book in Germany. Freud had read the work in manuscript but had advised Weininger against publication. See Vincent Brome, *Freud and his Early Circle*

(Heinemann, London, 1967), p. 9.

7. The *Freewoman* assumed a knowledge of Weininger's work on the part of its readers (1 February 1912, p. 216 and 8 February 1912, p. 235), and in one issue published an excerpt from *Sex and Character* (25 April 1912, pp. 452-5). Weininger was acknowledged to have given (albeit unconsciously) a description of the psychological processes underlying and accompanying women's exploited position. His more overt misogyny was passed over. See the editorial for 4 April 1912, pp. 381-2.

8. See Emile Delavenay, 'Sur un Exemplaire de Schopenhauer annoté par D.H. Lawrence', *Revue Anglo-Americaine*, vol. 13, no. 3 (1936), pp. 234-8, and Eleanor H. Green, 'Schopenhauer and D.H. Lawrence on Sex and Love', *D.H. Lawrence Review*, vol. 8, no. 3 (1975), pp. 329-45.

9. Cecil Gray, *Peter Warlock: A Memoir of Philip Heseltine* (Jonathan Cape, London, 1934), p. 67.

10. Ellis was a regular contributor to the *New Age*, which Lawrence read as a student, and the *Occult Review*, which he read during the war.

11. Mrs Oliphant, 'The Anti-Marriage League', *Blackwood's Magazine*, January 1896, pp. 135-49.

12. R.Y. Tyrrell, 'Jude the Obscure', *Fortnightly Review*, 1 June 1896, p. 857.

13. Havelock Ellis, 'Concerning *Jude the Obscure*', *Savoy*, October 1896, pp. 35-49. See also Ellis's article on 'Thomas Hardy's Novels', *Westminster Review*, 1 April 1883, pp. 334-64.

14. *Phoenix*, p. 444.

15. Ibid., p. 443.

16. Edward Carpenter, *Love's Coming-of-Age* (Labour Press, Manchester, 1896), p. 20.

17. Otto Weininger, *Sex and Character* (Heinemann, London, 1906), p. xi.

18. *Freewoman*, 16 May 1912, p. 505.

19. *Phoenix*, p. 402.

20. Ibid., p. 403.

21. Ibid., p. 410.

22. *Poems*, p. 219. The poem was probably written in 1913.

23. *Phoenix*, p. 441. Lawrence was not, however, an advocate of contraception. In a letter to Frieda written on 15 May 1912, shortly after their elopement, he says 'I do not believe, when people love each other, in interfering there. It is wicked, according to my feeling.' (*Letters*, vol. 1, pp. 402-3.) Nor, in this essentially theoretical discourse, does he discuss what an impediment to further self-realisation children might be to a woman who had to devote much of her time to caring for them; but the fate of Anna Brangwen in *The Rainbow* suggests he was not unaware of the issues involved.

24. Edward Carpenter, *The Drama of Love and Death* (George Allen, London, 1912), p. 59.

25. See for example 'The Objects of Marriage', *Birth Control Review*, June 1917, pp. 3-4 and 8, and 'The Love Rights of Woman', ibid., June 1918, pp. 3-6.

26. *Phoenix*, p. 481.

27. See A.J.L. Busst, 'The Image of the Androgyne in the Nineteenth Century', in Ian Fletcher (ed.), *Romantic Mythologies* (Routledge and Kegan Paul, London, 1967), pp. 1-95.

28. Fliess wrote to Freud in 1904, 'A book by Weininger has come to my attention in which I find, to my astonishment, my ideas on bisexuality and the consequent kind of sexual attraction — feminine men attract masculine women and vice versa — expounded in the first biological section. I see from one of the quotations that Weininger was in contact with Swoboda — your pupil — and I hear that the two men were very close friends. I have no doubt that Weininger

obtained knowledge of my ideas through you and that there was an abuse of other people's property on his part.' (Brome, *Freud and his Early Circle*, p. 7.)

29. Weininger, *Sex and Character*, p. 7.
30. Edward Carpenter, *The Intermediate Sex* (Swan Sonnenschein, London, 1908), p. 17.
31. Florence Farr, *Modern Woman: Her Intentions* (Frank Palmer, London, 1910), pp. 81-2.
32. Helen Corke, *In Our Infancy* (Cambridge University Press, Cambridge, 1975), pp. 210-11.
33. Weininger, *Sex and Character*, p. 35. Schopenhauer had postulated that 'the most manly man will desire the most womanly woman, and *vice versa*, and so each will want the individual that exactly corresponds to him in degree of sex.' (*Essays of Schopenhauer*, tr. Mrs Rudolf Dircks (Walter Scott, London, 1897), p. 188.)
34. *Phoenix*, p. 468.
35. Ibid., p. 443.
36. Ibid., p. 481.
37. Ibid., p. 514.
38. Weininger, *Sex and Character*, pp. 286 and 292.
39. Ibid., p. 111.
40. *Phoenix*, p. 459.
41. Havelock Ellis, *Man and Woman* (Walter Scott, London, 1894), pp. 297-8.
42. Ibid., p. 371.
43. Ibid., p. 326.
44. Ibid., p. 370.
45. Havelock Ellis, *The New Spirit* (George Bell, London, 1890), p. 9.
46. Carpenter, *Love's Coming-of-Age*, p. 40.
47. Ibid.
48. Ibid., pp. 50-2.
49. *Phoenix*, pp. 491-2.
50. Weininger, *Sex and Character*, p. 298.
51. See 'Lawrence's Quarrel with Freud' in Frederick Hoffman, *Freudianism and the Literary Mind* (Louisiana State University Press, Baton Rouge, 1945), Ch. 6 (pp. 149-80), for a general account of Lawrence's views on psychoanalysis. Barbara Low's book *Psycho-Analysis: A Brief Account of the Freudian Theory* (Allen and Unwin, London, 1920) is a possible source for Lawrence's knowledge of Freudianism. He was sought out by Freudians after the publication of the 'Oedipal' *Sons and Lovers* in 1913.
52. Letter of 21 November 1942, quoted in Hoffman, p. 153.
53. Frieda Lawrence, *Not I, But the Wind...* (Heinemann, London, 1935), p. 3.
54. Hoffman, *Freudianism and the Literary Mind*, p. 32.
55. Martin Green, *The Von Richthofen Sisters* (Weidenfeld and Nicolson, London, 1974), p. 11.
56. Ibid., p. 73.
57. Letter to Frieda Weekley, 16 May 1912. *Letters*, vol. 1, p. 404.
58. Letter to Katherine Mansfield, 21 November 1918. *Collected Letters*, p. 565.
59. Letter to Lady Cynthia Asquith, 7 February 1916. *Letters*, vol. 2, p. 526.
60. *Phoenix*, p. 621.
61. *Fantasia of the Unconscious*, p. 98.
62. Ibid., p. 18.
63. Ibid., pp. 100-1.
64. Ibid., p. 111.
65. Ibid., p. 96.
66. Ibid., p. 100.
67. Ibid., p. 97.
68. Ibid., p. 100.

5 MAN TO MAN

When Lawrence espoused patriarchy in the twenties he did not see himself as a reactionary, condoning the *status quo* and reinforcing a system that already flourished. For him, at this point, female dominance *was* to all intents and purposes the *status quo*, and male superiority was the urgent revolutionary movement necessary to restore things to their rightful order.

> All fights for freedom, that succeed, go too far, and become in turn the infliction of a tyranny. Like Napoleon or a soviet. And like the freedom of women. Perhaps the greatest revolution of modern times is the emancipation of women; and perhaps the deepest fight for two thousand years and more has been the fight for woman's independence, or freedom, call it what you will. The fight was deeply bitter, and, it seems to me, it is won. It is even going beyond, and becoming a tyranny of woman, of the individual woman in the house, and of the feminine ideas and ideals in the world.[1]

He believed society to be in a state of fatal confusion because it 'asserted . . . the life-centrality of woman'.[2] Such a belief may seem absurd — after all, women were quite obviously not dominant in society in any accepted sense of the word, although their position was certainly changing fast — and it is easy to simply ascribe a personal paranoia about female dominance to Lawrence. Other men, however, shared his feelings. One writer, looking back over the post-war decade in 1930, concluded that 'the nineteen-twenties was in a special sense the woman's decade',[3] while in the same year another commentator noted what he called 'the social supremacy of women'. 'It is their world,' he declared. 'They set the pace.'[4]

How far were such feelings justified? There is no doubt that women's war-work had been instrumental in removing many restrictions and prejudices. Maude Royden wrote in 1917:

> Woman, who could prove nothing by showing that she could do her own very necessary work, has convinced even the vanity of man by showing that she can do his. A woman who bore a child or many children, ran a household, and brought up a family fit and virtuous,

was still only 'arrested man,' and a perpetual minor; but a woman who can clip tickets on a tramcar is recognised at once as a Superwoman — in other words, a man.[5]

There is evidence of an upsurge in self-confidence and purposiveness among women at this time, acquired during war-work and sealed by the granting of the vote to those over 30 in 1918. Lawrence wrote in 1928 of women's 'unloosed energy';[6] the popular writer Philip Gibbs remarks:

> Before they were done with in that war, many of them had departed from all the traditions of their previous life and from centuries of history that had kept womanhood behind the window blinds. They were out and away in this new freedom.[7]

Many men, on the other hand, were demoralised by the brutality and futility of the war. Those who survived it, a large number of whom were physically or psychologically mutilated, returned to a society where they were 'in the minority, overwhelmed by numbers'.[8] The 1921 census revealed 1,095 women to every 1,000 men, with the greatest discrepancy occurring amongst the relatively young, where the largest proportion of the men had been eligible for active service.[9] Furthermore, men faced the additional problem of unemployment throughout the decade. It affected women too, of course, but on the whole a greater proportion of them than before were earning their own living, despite attempts to close to them the temporary employment opportunities that the war had provided. It was also during this period that women first began to exercise control over their own fertility on a large scale, to tentatively acknowledge and assert their own sexuality, and to use their new political power to institute reform in matters that particularly concerned them. To a patriarchy whose ideology had received a severe battering in the war, it is not difficult to see how it could begin to appear that women, if not dominant, were at least more powerful than ever before.

Lawrence believed that women had become the 'life-managers' of society, and that, as a consequence, domestic and ultimately trivial concerns were beginning to dominate politics. He implies that the growth of capitalism and industrialisation have been the result of the female domination of society: 'the triumph of the productive and domestic activities of man over all his previous military or adventurous or flaunting activities is a triumph of the woman in the home.'[10] He saw the ideology of progress, reform and humanitarianism as a spurious feminine ideology which he blamed for most of society's problems. The emergence of this complex of hostilities in Lawrence's writing seems to be linked with the emergence of what came to be known as 'New Feminism' ('Social Feminism' in the USA) as a force in political life.

In the immediate post-war years, there was a 'flurry of legislative activity on behalf of women'.[11] Suffragists had always argued that, if granted political power, they would use it to bring about improvements in those areas of life specifically relevant to women or traditionally designated feminine, and hence often ignored by male legislators — questions affecting maternity, child care, health, housing, food and so on. To a large extent this was indeed the direction taken by the organised feminist movements in the twenties. *The Woman's Year Book* for 1923-4, compiled by the National Union of Societies for Equal Citizenship, which united many of the old moderate suffrage groups, listed fourteen acts passed since the end of the war which demonstrated 'the influence of the women's vote'.[12] The 1920s was a period of post-war reconstruction, and feminism too now became predominantly progressive, reformist and welfare-oriented.

> Whereas the main current of late nineteenth century feminism had been to demand access into the world controlled by men by demanding equal rights at work, in education, and the vote, from the early twentieth century women began to concentrate more on biological and domestic oppression . . . They made demands for better maternity provision, protection at work, family allowances, and sometimes for birth control and abortion. Theoretically they were beginning to consider the significance of women's domestic labour, the consequences of birth control and procreation, the importance of child psychology and children's education.[13]

The New Feminism, whose principal spokeswoman during the twenties was Eleanor Rathbone, was no longer committed to simple egalitarianism, but rather to a society which acknowledged and catered for women's special needs. Rathbone declared that the time had come to 'demand what we want for women, not because it is what men have got, but because it is what women need to fulfil the potentialities of their own natures'.[14] This potentially radical formulation tended in fact to peter out in ineffective reforms, but its effect should not be underestimated, particularly on men who for the first time became aware of topics such as the endowment of motherhood being seriously discussed in a political context. Feminists were now elevating the traditional female roles of wife and mother to a level of real — as opposed to merely sentimental — equality and importance with men's role. This must have appeared as threatening to men as the earlier type of femininism which had aimed to 'invade' the male world.

At the same time, a sexual revolution was taking place. Women in the twenties were beginning to exercise more control over their sexuality and reproductive powers. Dora Russell said of the pre-war feminist movement that it 'dared not cry out that women had bodies. Its one hope of success was to prove that women had minds.' But post-war feminism, she believed, had a different character: its important task was to 'accept and proclaim sex'.[15] The increased frankness about sexuality is well exemplified by the eccentric career of Marie Stopes. Although primarily remembered as a campaigner for family planning, the original theme of *Married Love*, published in 1918, was the consistent denial or ignoring of female sexuality and the unhappiness which this caused. The book encouraged women to assert their sexual needs, and Stopes's rhetoric was probably not excessive when she wrote that

> the main ideas in the book crashed into English society like a bombshell. Its explosively contagious main theme — that woman like man has the same physiological reaction, a reciprocal need for enjoyment and benefit from sex union in marriage distinct from the exercise of maternal functions — made Victorian husbands gasp.[16]

Stopes realised that many women were so alienated from their own sexuality that they had to be taught the most basic facts about their bodies. To those who suggested that such matters could be safely left to instinct, she replied that 'instinct is *not* enough',[17] and this attitude dominated the fields of sex education, motherhood and child care in the twenties. The reactions of feminists to Stopes were mixed; Naomi Mitchison wrote in 1930, criticising Lawrence's censure of Stopes in *Pornography and Obscenity*, that '*Married Love* was a light in great darkness to many of us, though a light shining through a lantern which was possibly not in the best taste.'[18] But contraception made great inroads into public acceptability in the twenties. In 1925 the National Union of Societies for Equal Citizenship adopted it as part of its reform programme, and by 1930 Mitchison could write that it was 'taken for granted as a good, and as something essential to real civilization'.[19] Inevitably, to some degree, the concept of the right of women to have control over their own bodies must also have gained currency, and such a concept might well have added to male insecurity. In addition, the twenties produced scientific developments which seemed to threaten the *status quo* of reproduction. One of the most controversial aspects of Marie Stopes's trial centred around her advocacy of artificial insemination for women whose husbands were infertile,[20] while at the same time J.B.S. Haldane (Naomi Mitchison's brother) was prophesying artificial reproduction, or 'ectogenesis'.[21]

Paradoxically, while feminists were tending to change the emphasis of their campaigns during the twenties towards issues which affected women specifically as women, it must have seemed to the superficial observer that women were discarding the traditional paraphernalia of femininity. In the immediate post-war years the image of women changed radically and they became 'sophisticated to an extent which was revolutionary when compared with the romantic ignorance of 1914'.[22] The flapper, the representative of this youthful sophistication, became a symbol for the decade. The adoption of short skirts and short hair, and the participation by young women in the life-style of the 'Roaring Twenties', constituted one kind of liberation. It was only superficial, but nevertheless it, too, 'struck horror into the patriarchal soul'.[23]

There were thus two contradictory elements contributing to male fears about women in the twenties. The first was that political and social life would become swamped by female concerns, that there would be a state of 'petticoat government': the second, that women were losing their femininity and becoming more like men, and that the security of the traditional sexual roles was becoming blurred. Both feelings combined in a general fear of emasculation.

In his book *Since Then*, Philip Gibbs devotes a substantial chapter to what he calls 'the unveiling of women'. Gibbs was a popular writer who was usually in tune with contemporary feeling; Q.D. Leavis described him as typical of 'the novelists to whom the general public go for help and advice'.[24] Before the war he had written a 'suffragette novel', *Intellectual Mansions*, and during the war a study of women's warwork. In his survey of the twenties he sympathises, in general terms, with women's emancipation. He notes with approval that 'it is the mind of modern women — these post-war women — which is at work in civilisation today, razing old foundations of tradition, altering the code of conduct, taking the lead in social reform',[25] a sentiment which echoes Lawrence's assertion that women have become the 'lifemanagers' of society. But Gibbs also reveals a deep fear of emasculation with regard to women's changing position. 'They set the pace, some of these girls, and the boys can't keep up with them ... Nature gives with one hand and takes with another. If women become more masculine, men must become more feminine — a serious and depressing thought!'[26] Gibbs can only see the process of emancipation as one of becoming more masculine, without stopping to question traditional cultural definitions of masculinity and femininity. He is worried that the new behaviour of women, exciting and even necessary as it may seem, is 'unnatural'. 'Is it going to make a better and a more beautiful world, or is it a challenge against Nature itself, a sign of some decadence overtaking humanity because man, enfeebled and overwhelmed, is surrendering his natural rights and privileges?'[27] Despite attempting to be impartial, Gibbs cannot banish his fear

> that men are losing as women are gaining, and that the natural balance of the sexes and their biological relationship are being thwarted by the claims of women who are becoming unsexed, anarchical and rebellious against natural laws, while man, weakly acquiescing in his own destruction, is becoming emasculated, decadent and doomed.[28]

Similar views are expressed by A.M. Ludovici in a series of books whose arguments are very close to those of Lawrence.[29] In *Woman: A Vindication*, published in the same year as *Fantasia of the Unconscious*, Ludovici argues that 'modern society is . . . thoroughly and deeply saturated with feminist prejudices and ideas',[30] and that 'Feminism is undeniably a phenomenon of male degeneration'.[31] Like Lawrence, Ludovici sees Christianity, democracy, industrialisation and feminism as linked evils, and in *Lysistrata* he defines the feminist movement as an 'offshoot of the body-despising values'.[32] He attributes the rise of feminism to 'a marked decline in the ability, versatility and masculinity of men',[33] to which the solution is a masculine renaissance and a new breed of manly men:

> The highest type of this kind of manly man is the ruler who gives us a new order and a new goal; while even the lowest type is the husband who fills a woman's life and whom she finds it a joy to obey and no indignity, no hardship to serve.[34]

These attitudes are consolidated in *Man: An Indictment*, where Ludovici again analyses the causes of feminism — 'in this male degeneracy must be sought the common cause for both the emancipation of the female and the decline of the civilization in which she becomes emancipated'[35] — and sets out 'the only profitable and genuine remedy, a regeneration of men'.[36]

> Only in this masculine renaissance is there any hope of a revival for humanity as a whole. And as soon as the men appear who will constitute this rebirth of desirable male material, everything will be bound to fall naturally into its proper place. The relation of the sexes will immediately recover its serenity, beauty and elevation.[37]

Vera Brittain writes of the 'post-war reaction, in which war neurosis had been transformed into fear — fear especially of incalculable results following from unforeseen causes; fear of the loss of power by those in possession of it; fear, therefore, of women'.[38] Much of Lawrence's later writing appears to spring from such insecurity.[39] Like other male writers in the twenties, he declaims against the confusion of sexual roles, the masculinisation of women and the corresponding effeminacy of men; he questions women's attempts to enter the male world, especially politics; and he contrasts the new 'scientific' attitudes towards sexuality, maternity and child-rearing with the 'instinctive' behaviour of the past. These assumptions about changing sexual roles underlie and account for Lawrence's exploration of male power and male comradeship in *Aaron's Rod, Kangaroo*, and *The Plumed Serpent*. They are set out most explicitly in the non-fiction writing of the twenties, especially in *Fantasia of the Unconscious*.

Most of the views on sex roles in *Fantasia of the Unconscious* spring from Lawrence's conviction, mentioned at the beginning of this chapter, that he was living in a matriarchy, and thus in an age of sexual confusion. Men, according to Lawrence, are 'naturally' creatures of action, energy and authority, while women are emotional, intuitive and sympathetic. But this natural division has become distorted as the result of the predominance of an ethic of Christian benevolence and liberal idealism.

> Our ideal has taught us to be *so* loving and *so* submissive and *so* yielding in our sympathy that the mode has become automatic in many men. Now in what we will call the 'natural' mode, man has his positivity in the volitional centres, and woman in the sympathetic. In fulfilling the Christian love ideal, however, men have reversed this. Man has assumed the gentle, all-sympathetic role, and woman has become the energetic party, with the authority in her hands. The male is the sensitive, sympathetic nature, the woman is

the active, effective, authoritative.[40]

In other words, men have become effeminate and women masculine. But a natural polarity can never be completely reversed, although it may be travestied; and women's 'unnatural' energy and authority is nevertheless exercised in the service of their 'natural' functions of sex and maternity. This appears to be a direct reference to the New Feminism and its policy of campaigning through constitutional channels for reform in matters specifically relevant to women. Men, Lawrence argues, retain some of their capacity for authority and activity, but these are increasingly devoted to 'the great end of Woman, wife and mother'.[41] The male animal, he felt, was becoming domesticated and accepting a feminine scale of values.

> Now his activity is all of the domestic order and all his thought goes to proving that nothing matters except that birth shall continue and woman shall rock the nest of the globe like a bird who covers her eggs in some tall tree.[42]

Lawrence is fiercely hostile to this state of affairs and to the ethos of humanism, liberalism and progress which he sees as responsible for it. The Brave New World of the Welfare State is anathema to him.

> We have made a mistake, laying down love like the permanent way of a great emotional transport system. There we are, however, running on wheels on the lines of our love . . . 'Onward, Christian soldiers, towards the great terminus where bottles of sterilized milk for the babies are delivered at the bedroom windows by noiseless aeroplanes each morn, where the science of dentistry is so perfect that teeth are planted in a man's mouth without his knowing it, where twilight sleep is so delicious that every woman longs for her next confinement, and where nobody ever has to do anything except turn a handle now and then in a spirit of universal love –' That is the forward direction of the English-speaking race.[43]

To correct this drift, Lawrence proceeds to redefine politics as a male activity from which women are to be excluded – at a moment in history when women were at last beginning to enter politics and influence political decisions. He had, of course, earlier urged the involvement of women in politics to legislate on matters that concerned them – precisely the policy of the New Feminism. In 1915, for example, he had written that 'women *must* govern such things as the feeding and housing of the race . . . women shall have absolutely equal voices with regard to marriage, custody of children etc.'[44] But when the reality materialised, he seems to have found it a threat. In *Fantasia of the Unconscious* he asserts that it is the predominant desire of men – and *only* of men – to 'build a world', to 'live for ever from an inherent sense of *purpose*'.[45] Women should keep to their 'separate sphere' of feeling and sympathy. They exist 'in the twilight, by the camp fire, when day has departed'.[46] Lawrence warns men that when they vacate the positions of power that are theirs by divine right, women take over, trivialising power and turning it into a farce. 'Once man vacates this strong citadel of his own genuine, not spurious, divinity, then in comes woman, picks up the sceptre and begins to conduct a rag-time band.'[47] Lawrence reserves a particular hostility for the scientific approach to sexuality and motherhood, and especially for modern methods of child-rearing.

> A relation between mother and child today is practically *never* parental . . . The mother, in her new role of idealist and life-manager, never, practically for one single moment, gives her child the unthinking response from the deep dynamic centres. No, she gives it what is good for it. She shoves milk in its mouth as the clock strikes, she shoves it to sleep when the milk is swallowed, and she shoves it ideally through baths and massage, promenades and practice, till the little organism develops like a mushroom to stand on its own feet. Then she continues her ideal shoving of it through all the stages of an ideal upbringing, she loves it as a chemist loves his test-tubes.[48]

In *Fantasia of the Unconscious* Lawrence consistently asserts that paternity is as important as maternity. Along with his rejection of 'scientific' motherhood goes a vehement opposition to sexual education of any kind, not only for children – 'it is ten times criminal to tell young children facts about sex'[49] – but for adults as well:

> Sex should come upon us as a terrible thing of suffering and privilege and mystery: a mysterious metamorphosis come upon us, and a new terrible power given us, and a new responsibility. Telling? What's the good of telling? The mystery, the terror, and the tremendous power of sex should never be explained away. The mass of mankind should *never* be acquainted with the scientific biological facts of sex: *never*.[50]

As for the superficial emancipation of women that was a characteristic of the twenties, and their access to types of life-style previously reserved for men, Lawrence believed that it was merely part of the larger cultural phenomenon of an unnatural role-reversal, and, as such, would ultimately be found to be sterile and disappointing. In 'Laura Philippine' (1928)[51] he sketches the aimless liberation of the flapper whose life is a succession of cocktails and dances; more seriously, he writes in *Fantasia of the Unconscious* of

> a race of 'intelligent' women, delightful companions, tricky courtesans, clever prostitutes, noble idealists, devoted friends, interesting mistresses, efficient workers, brilliant managers, women as good as men at all the manly tricks: and better, because they are so very headlong once they go in for men's tricks. But then, after a while, pop it all goes. The moment woman has got man's ideals and tricks drilled into her, the moment she is competent in the manly world — there's an end of it. She's had enough . . . She hates the thing she has embraced. She becomes absolutely perverse, and her one end is to prostitute herself and her ideals to sex. Which is her business at the present moment.[52]

Lawrence believed that women only sought emancipation when men abdicated from their responsibilities — to fill a vacuum, as it were. In 'The Real Thing' he claims that when women appear to be struggling for their freedom, they are in fact struggling against men who are no longer 'real' men. At certain periods in history 'Man loses his faith in himself, and woman begins to fight him.'[53] This point of view is expounded elsewhere, most notably in the discussion of *The Scarlet Letter* in *Studies in Classic American Literature* (1923), where Lawrence asserts that 'woman is the nemesis of doubting man'.[54] The women's movement is seen as a destructive force based on unconscious revenge against men for having left women in the lurch. 'Revenge! REVENGE! It is this that fills the unconscious spirit of woman today. Revenge against man, and against the spirit of man, which has betrayed her into unbelief.'[55] The solution to the problem can only lie with men reasserting their masculinity. 'When is the fight over? Ah when! Modern life seems to give no answer. Perhaps when a man finds his strength and his rooted belief in himself again.'[56]

The conviction that female emancipation arises from men's loss of faith in their own masculinity is thus the primary impetus behind Lawrence's exploration of male bonding and male power in *Aaron's*

Rod, *Kangaroo* and *The Plumed Serpent*. In contrast to the dogmatism of the essays, however, the novels remain explorations, and rather tentative ones at that. Lawrence's ultimate failure to be convinced by his own new theories is honestly set down in these novels; nowhere do we see the male comradeship and the male power which are talked of convincingly realised. His wavering allegiance and the impression that he is groping somewhat wildly for a set of values to sustain him in the nightmare of the post-war world contribute partly to the dubious quality of much of the writing of this period. Lawrence was later to find such a set of values, and a corresponding recovery of some sort of poise in his writing, in the cult of the phallus.

Aaron's Rod is a novel about masculinist consciousness-raising, and as such is a kind of mirror-image of the traditional feminist novel in which the heroine escapes from an unhappy marriage or a repressive family and embarks on a process of self-discovery in an alien, male-dominated world. The men in *Aaron's Rod* live in a society which seems to them to be ruled by the other sex and its values. They feel that women have arrogated all sexual initiative and that their own function has been eroded to that of mere progenitor. They are isolated from the majority of their fellow men, who have internalised their own oppression and accepted the prevailing feminine values.

Female characters in *Aaron's Rod* are conspicuously absent. Aaron leaves his wife at the beginning of the novel and his subsequent sexual encounters with women are always preludes to disaster. After sleeping with Josephine Ford, he is taken seriously ill. 'I felt, the minute I was loving her, I'd done myself . . . I felt it go, inside me, the minute I gave in to her. It's perhaps killed me.'[57] And after a meeting with the Marchesa later in the novel, he is robbed.

> Yes — and if I hadn't rushed along so full of feeling: if I hadn't exposed myself: if I hadn't got worked up with the Marchesa, and then rushed all kindled through the streets, without reserve: it would never have happened. I gave myself away: and there was someone ready to snatch what I gave.[58]

However, it is hard for Aaron to abandon the idea of seeking confirmation of his masculinity through sexual potency with women, and it takes some time for him to be converted to Lilly's position, the familiar Lawrentian one of singleness and self-sufficiency preceding any attempt at relationship. The novel suggests that the relations between the sexes have gone so disastrously wrong that it is better, for the present, to stand aloof from the fray.

It is Lilly's thesis that there are two 'great dynamic urges'[59] in life, love and power, and that our culture has based itself too exclusively on the former, with appalling consequences. Diatribes against love, idealism, humanitarianism, benevolence and the relinquishing of independence and self-control recur throughout the novel, and are consistently linked to attacks on the elevation of femininity and motherhood. Aaron complains:

> When a woman's got her children, by God, she's a bitch in the manger . . . they look on a man as if he was nothing but an instrument to get and rear children . . . Is my life given me for nothing but to get children, and work for a woman?[60]

Lilly endorses Aaron's anger, but tries to steer the argument towards the necessity for men to bond together against female oppression.

> And can you find two men to stick together, without feeling criminal, and without cringing, and without betraying one another? You can't. One is sure to go fawning round some female, then they both enjoy giving each other away, and doing a new grovel before a woman again.[61]

The novel offers an analysis of Aaron's marriage to a woman who has been led to believe that 'she, as woman, was the centre of creation, the man was but an adjunct. She, as woman, and particularly as mother, was the first great source of life and being, and also of culture.'[62]

> Sure enough, Lottie had never formulated this belief inside herself. But it was formulated for her in the whole world. It is the substantial and professed belief of the whole white world. She did but inevitably represent what the whole world around her asserted: the life-centrality of woman.[63]

But Aaron is a rebel, ripe for conversion to masculinism. In the famous exchange with Aaron on which the book ends, Lilly urges 'the deep, fathomless submission to the heroic soul in a greater man'[64] and a change from the mode of love to the mode of power. It is clear that this entails a change in the relationship between the sexes as well as between men themselves. 'The woman must submit . . . not to any foolish fixed authority, not to any foolish and arbitrary will . . . No subservience.

None of that. No slavery. A deep, unfathomable free submission.'[65] This voluntary submission on the part of women is also prophesied in *Studies in Classic American Literature*, which belongs to the same period, and portrayed, but never without unease and ambiguity, in *The Fox* and *The Captain's Doll*, and in *The Plumed Serpent*.

Transpose the sexes of the characters in *Aaron's Rod*, and it becomes a novel in a recognisable tradition, familiar to anyone who is acquainted with the fiction that has come out of the feminist movement. Interestingly, the criticisms most commonly levelled at it are also those criticisms frequently made of feminist novels − it is didactic, hysterical, lacking in humour, and its preoccupations seem slightly absurd to anyone who does not share the writer's (distorted) viewpoint.

In *Kangaroo* Lawrence treats more fully the need for men to come together as a political force. Somers, a natural outsider, takes a decision to become politically involved, and the novel charts his experiments with various political factions in post-war Australia.[66] Somers is adamant that his new venture is to be exclusively masculine: 'he insisted . . . that the pure male activity should be womanless, beyond woman'.[67] Jack Callcott, who introduces Somers to the Diggers, confirms the all-male nature of the group. 'We're not having the women in, if we can help it.'[68] Amongst both the Socialists and the proto-fascist Diggers, there is a strong emphasis on male comradeship (the word Jack uses is 'mate'). He asks Somers to be his 'mate', but Somers feels unable to commit himself. Later in the novel Somers is deeply moved when Willie Struthers, the socialist leader, asks him to write for a paper whose aim will be to unite the working class on a similar basis of comradeship. This male solidarity is envisaged as superseding the attachment to wife and family which at present divides working men from each other. 'It was to be the new tie between men, in the new democracy. It was to be the new passional bond in the new society. The trusting love of a man for his mate.'[69] Somers prefers this brand of socialism to any purely materialist political theory, but he is still unable to commit himself politically. 'It all seemed so far from the dark God he wished to serve.'[70]

Somers's repeated disillusionment with political organisations is based on his discovery that they are all founded on the concept of love, which he feels has played itself out. At first, Kangaroo seems to offer what Somers is looking for, with his assertion that the only viable form of political organisation is 'strong, just power from above'.[71] Yet even in Kangaroo Somers finds a commitment to the principle of love, and it is this which finally disconcerts him. Given the all-male composition of the Diggers, their ideal of a benevolent autocracy can hardly be explicitly associated with femininity. But Kangaroo himself is an androgynous, at times almost maternal figure, whose body is composed of 'roundnesses and downward-dropping heaviness'.[72] 'You felt you were cuddled cosily, like a child, on his breast, in the soft glow of his heart, and that your feet were nestling on his ample, beautiful "tummy".'[73] This aspect of Kangaroo is so disturbing that William James, referring to his broad thighs and round stomach, comments to Somers, 'He's not quite the *shape* of a man that I should throw away my eyes for.'[74]

Lawrence shows Somers's real convictions — if he can be said to have any, for he clings tenaciously to a distrust of the absolute — evolving only slowly and tentatively from his dissatisfaction with the political options open to him. *Kangaroo* is a catalogue of ideas tested and found wanting, and Somers is constantly revising what he thinks he believes in. What emerges is still a commitment to hierarchy as opposed to democracy, but not a hierarchy of love.

> Perhaps . . . the mystery of lordship. The mystery of innate, natural, sacred priority. The other mystic relationship between men, which democracy and equality try to deny and obliterate. Not any arbitrary caste or birth aristocracy. But the mystic recognition of difference and innate priority, the joy of obedience and the sacred responsibility of authority.[75]

Somers counters Kangaroo's insistence on love with his theory of the dark god who 'enters us from below, not from above . . . from the lower self, the dark self, the phallic self, if you like'.[76]

Faced with the impossibility of finding a context for his beliefs amongst the political groups who court him, Somers turns back to his personal relationship with Harriet, as she had predicted he would, and attempts to put his ideas on dominance into practice there. The chapter entitled 'Harriet and Lovat at Sea in Marriage' may be, as Eliseo Vivas has commented, 'pure *corn*',[77] an example of Lawrence's style at its very worst. But it does at least betray the absurdity of Somers's desire to be 'lord and master' in his marriage, and Lawrence's inabilty to offer it for serious consideration. From what the novel has told us of Somers, the reader is likely to find the idea as ridiculous as Harriet does.

Him, a lord and master! Why, he was not really lord of his own

bread and butter; next year they might both be starving. And he
was not even master of himself, with his ungovernable furies and
his uncritical intimacies with people . . .

All he could do was to try and come it over her with this revolution rubbish and a stunt of 'male' activity. If it were even real!

He had nothing but her, absolutely. And that was why, presumably, he wanted to establish this ascendancy over her, assume this arrogance.[78]

As this passage illustrates, Lawrence gives full play in the novel to Somers's inconsistencies. This prophet of masculinity is hopelessly dependent not only upon his wife but upon the memory of his mother. Moreover, the disciple of the 'dark god' becomes a sudden puritan when Victoria Callcot seems to be offering herself to him sexually, and is 'frankly disturbed' by the freedom of the Callcotts' relationship, 'not liking the thought of applying the same prescription to his own marriage'.[79]

Yet despite Somers's absurdities, we *are* asked to take seriously the proposition that, given a spiritual change in men themselves, the establishment of the sexual and social hierarchies which Somers desires might come about.

He did not yet submit to the fact which he *half* knew: that before mankind would accept any man for a king, and before Harriet would ever accept him, Richard Lovat, as a lord and master, he, the selfsame Richard who was so strong on kingship, must open the doors of his soul and let in a dark Lord and Master for himself, the dark god he had sensed outside the door.[80]

In *The Plumed Serpent*[81] Lawrence attempts to define the 'dark god', the religious answer which has come to replace any merely social or political solution to the problems with which he is concerned. The changes in presentation in the three novels under discussion are interesting. In *Aaron's Rod* the man with the theories on power appears as a guru to the spiritually lost Aaron, who is a novice, a neophyte still engaged in masculinist consciousness-raising and in extricating himself from relationships with women. In *Kangaroo* the same character has become the centre of consciousness in the novel, which then develops into a psychomachia in which his doubts, hesitations and inconsistencies are dramatised. But in *The Plumed Serpent* Lawrence takes a woman for his central character, although ideologically the novel is a continuation of *Kangaroo* in that it tries to actualise Somers's 'dark god'. Regardless of its content, it is generally agreed that the quality of the writing in *The Plumed Serpent* is higher than in the previous two novels. Lawrence appears to feel more confident portraying man-to-man relationships and masculine power from the outside, with a woman as the subject through whom the reader experiences them. At the same time there are now two spokesmen for this male power, Ramón and Cipriano, who emphasise the social and the sexual aspects respectively. The attempts of Ramón and Cipriano to start a spiritual revolution in Mexico, organised around the ancient cult of Quetzalcoatl, are seen through Kate's eyes, and the psychological interest of the novel lies in Kate's love-hate relationship with Mexico and with the particular brand of machismo with which it comes to be associated.

Ramón's campaign aims to restore to the Mexicans pride in their manhood, replacing a spurious liberty by a deep obedience, and an emasculated Jesus by a phallic Quetzalcoatl — for the plumed serpent is 'the snake of the body'.[82]

> I will serve the God that gives me my manhood. There is no liberty for a man, apart from the God of his manhood. Free Mexico is a bully, and the old, colonial, ecclesiastical Mexico was another sort of bully. When man has nothing but his *will* to assert — even his good-will — it is always bullying. Bolshevism is one sort of bullying, capitalism another: and liberty is a change of chains.[83]

The values against which Ramón is in revolt are partly represented in the novel by his first wife, Carlota. She symbolises the veneer of western civilisation which has been imposed on Mexico, an artificial female refinement overlaying its primitive masculinity. She is a European and a pious Catholic, dedicated to charity and good works. For her, the pride which Ramón has made the basis of the Quetzalcoatl cult is a sin: 'Don't you think it was just against this danger that Christ came, to teach men a proper humility?'[84] Christianity is defined in the novel as a female religion,[85] and is contrasted with the emphasis on masculinity in the Quetzalcoatl revival. Carlota's is a religion of love, but we are told that the spontaneity of this love has gone, leaving only a willed charitableness and piety.

Carlota is also a maternal figure, the Magna Mater who sees men as wayward children and can therefore give no credence to their grandiose plans. Her husband's scheme is to her not only heretical madness, but, on another level, simply absurd. 'He — he — he wants to be worshipped.

To be worshipped! To be worshipped! A God! He whom I've held, I've held in my arms! He is a child, as all men are children.'[86] At the reopening of the church in Sayula as a temple of Quetzalcoatl, Carlota, the only person to openly protest, literally collapses on the altar of the new religion and later dies, its first sacrifice.

This part of the novel emphasises the fact that, although Lawrence is writing about Mexico, the basic themes are the same as those which preoccupied him in *Aaron's Rod* (set in England and Europe) and *Kangaroo* (set in Australia): namely, the need to eradicate a certain system of values designated 'female' and based on 'love', and to institute a new system designated 'male' and based on 'power'. For, despite Ramón's frequent references to 'womanhood' as well as 'manhood', his insistence on the presence of a woman in the new pantheon, and the celebration of a sacred marriage between Kate and Cipriano, the religious revolution is an essentially masculine affair. Kate muses that 'the highest thing this country might produce would be some powerful relationship of man to man',[87] and feels that the sexual relationship between men and women will always be secondary. But at the same time she thinks that 'when Cipriano said: *Man that is man is more than a man*, he seemed to be driving the male significance to its utmost, and beyond, with a sort of demonism.'[88] Women, she realises, have no real place in Ramón's campaign. 'Where was woman, in this terrible interchange of will? Truly only a subservient, instrumental thing: the soft stone on which the man sharpened the knife of his relentless volition.'[89] The phallicism of the Quetzalcoatl cult is dealt with in the next chapter in the discussion of Lawrence's last works, for we see in *The Plumed Serpent* the beginning of a return to a preoccupation with the relationship between men and women rather than that between men and men. The centre of interest in the novel shifts from the political and social plans of Ramón to the relationship between Kate and Cipriano, where Lawrence explores the voluntary return to submission by women which he had prophesied in *Aaron's Rod* and *Kangaroo*.

Kate is a woman of middle age, with two marriages behind her, one to a conventional bourgeois husband and one to an Irish political activist. She is presented as an emancipated and independent woman of the world, yet she is tired of her aimless freedom and ready for something new. On one level she is, in other words, an allegorical character in Lawrence's private mythology — a representation of the state which he believed twentieth-century western woman had reached, and which is described in *Fantasia of the Unconscious* and elsewhere. There he claims that women, having gained their freedom and cast off the restrictions of bourgeois morality, will toy with the 'man's world' of rational and political activity, will learn all the 'manly tricks' — but that ultimately they will find this unsatisfying and cast around for a different type of fulfilment. Kate, sick of Europe and her old way of life, has already reached this point. 'She felt she could cry aloud, for the unknown gods to put the magic back into her life, and to save her from the dry-rot of the world's sterility.'[90] Kate is however no feminist, but feels it better to 'stand faithfully behind a really brave man, than to push forward into the ranks of cheap and obtrusive women'.[91] She knows that she needs a relationship with a man, 'to stop the gap, and to keep her balanced'.[92] But most men, like her cousin Owen and his friend Villiers, who appear at the beginning of the novel, are hopelessly out of the question. The alternative that presents itself is the Quetzalcoatl cult and the type of relationship offered by Cipriano, which alternately attracts and repels Kate. The novel becomes a study of her vacillations between the old and the new worlds. Kate believes that 'till men are men indeed, women have no hope to be women'[93] — and with Ramón and Cipriano she feels, for the first time, 'in the presence of men'.[94] The rich physical beauty of the Mexican men also attracts her, yet at the same time she finds the assertion of the 'old male prerogative'[95] in them ridiculous. The conflict between these two sides of her personality is never fully resolved: in the last pages she is still hesitant, planning a return to Europe. Lawrence gives ample weight to Kate's periodic rejections of the Quetzalcoatl ethic, but it has been plausibly argued that 'the balancing of opposites breaks down and that the single beat of Quetzalcoatl's drum finally drowns out the sound of Kate's irreverent laughter'.[96] Her doubts are nearly always followed by a renewed desire to be convinced. To take one example of Lawrence's method: as soon as we have been shown Kate submitting sexually to Cipriano, Ramón's new bride Teresa is introduced, as if to put Kate's submission into perspective and show it as merely relative. Kate initially reacts with hostility to the relationship between Ramón and his second wife. 'Kate called it harem, and self-prostitution . . . surely it was the *slave* approach . . . Was it right? Kate asked herself. Wasn't it degrading for a woman?'[97] She congratulates herself that 'Her life was her own! It was not her *métier* to be fanning the blood in a man, to make him almighty and blood-glamorous.'[98] Yet she comes to envy Teresa, and the two women become friends. Kate is even forced to realise that Teresa might be in some way superior to her.

Yes, Kate was accustomed to looking on other women as inferiors. But the tables were suddenly turned . . . suddenly she had to question herself, whether Teresa was not a greater woman than she . . . Perhaps for the first time in her life she quailed and felt abashed: repentant.[99]

Kate's doubts are constantly undercut in this way. Ramón's two wives, Carlota and Teresa, can in fact be seen as representing, in exaggerated form, the two aspects of Kate which are in conflict throughout the novel. Just as Carlota dies and Teresa takes her place, so it is the submissive Kate, the bride of Huitzilpochtli, who triumphs in the end, although not without much struggle and many reservations. Her submission is not really the voluntary one that Lawrence had predicted in his earlier works. It is something achieved *faute de mieux*, against her better judgement, and the last words of the novel are Kate's to Cipriano: 'You won't let me go!'[100]

There are instances outside the three full-length novels of this period where Lawrence avoids making the malaise of post-war civilisation sex-specific. *St Mawr*, in its avoidance of the clichéd answer, is a much more accomplished and flexible work than any of the novels. Its theme is the problem of there being no 'real men' in the world — Mrs Witt and her daughter Lou are both, in their different ways, strong women for whom contemporary men are pitifully inadequate. Despite the fact that Mrs Witt is more or less a collection of all the characteristics that Lawrence professed to dislike in women, no criticism is offered of the strong-willed, sardonic American, with her cynicism and her probing, analytical mind. Her honesty, her readiness to change and to admit that she might have been wrong, her desire to wrest real meaning from her life and for death itself to be a real experience for her, all this vindicates her. She in fact dominates the story, and Lawrence allows her natural superiority to the other characters to shine through unimpeded.

Both Mrs Witt and Lou have had high expectations of their menfolk which can never be fulfilled. Mrs Witt knows that 'men were never really her match. A woman of terrible strong health, she felt even that in her strong limbs there was far more electric power than in the limbs of any man she had met.'[101] Lou muses, 'I only wish, with all my soul, that some men *were* bigger and stronger and *deeper* than I am . . .',[102] but knows that she has never found one who was. At the beginning of the novella, mother and daughter, united in their contempt for the men around them, nevertheless disagree about what qualities are to be most admired in a man. Lou, through St Mawr, is already convinced of the importance of the animal. 'A pure animal man would be as lovely as a deer or a leopard, burning like a flame fed straight from underneath.'[103] Mrs Witt at first clings to her preference for the intellect, although admitting that men whose minds she can admire no longer seem to exist. But the two women are brought closer together by the discussion about Pan, and the realisation that the impossibility, which they both desire, is to 'see Pan in a man'.[104]

The two men in the novel who are outsiders, Lewis, the Welsh groom, and Phoenix, Mrs Witt's tame Indian, have a glimmer of this Pan-like quality which the women recognise. Each woman contemplates the possibility of a relationship with one of these men. Mrs Witt goes as far as to ask Lewis to marry her, while Lou is momentarily tempted by Phoenix. But even these men are hopelessly inadequate for women of the calibre of Lou and her mother. Both are servants, and to some extent warped by the circumstances of their lives. Lou is honest with herself. 'She had no desire at all to fool herself into thinking that a Phoenix might be a husband and a mate.'[105] Instead, she turns away from relationship altogether, to a self-sufficiency which she characterises as virginity. 'My dealings with men have only broken my stillness and messed up my doorways.'[106] To Lewis she confides: 'It seems to me men and women have really hurt one another so much nowadays that they had better stay apart till they have learned to be gentle with one another again.'[107]

In *St Mawr*, the answer to what Lawrence saw as the problems of western society in the aftermath of the First World War is not conceived in terms of a reassertion of male power; nor is a return to the primitive in sexual terms suggested; nor are the aspects of modern life which Lawrence dislikes branded 'feminine' or attributed to female dominance. A certain type of emancipation — that of Flora Manby, who has read H.G. Wells and thinks that 'this is the best age there ever was for a girl to have a good time in'[108] — is still condemned, but Lawrence does not argue that a male counter-revolution is the solution.

The theme of male comradeship which occupies a central place in Lawrence's post-war work is thus more complicated than is usually suggested. In *Women in Love*, the relationship which Birkin envisages, but never really achieves, with Gerald, is conceived of as something complementary to his relationship with Ursula, a parallel to the close affection which exists between the two sisters. By the time of the composition of *Aaron's Rod*, however, Lawrence, in response to historical developments,[109] has developed a theory which asserts that women are now dominant, and that men have allowed the natural order to be overturned. Against this background, 'male comradeship ... becomes more clearly a banding together against women'.[110] It is a political act, a rallying call to men to shake off their apathy and assert their divine right of dominance.

Notes

1. 'The Real Thing', *Phoenix*, p. 196.
2. *Aaron's Rod*, p. 192.
3. A.C. Ward, *The 1920s: Literature and Ideas in the Post-War Decade* (Methuen, London, 1930), pp. 23-4.
4. Philip Gibbs, *Since Then* (Heinemann, London, 1930), p. 373.
5. A. Maude Royden, 'The Future of the Woman's Movement' in Victor Gollancz (ed.), *The Making of Women: Oxford Essays in Feminism* (Allen and Unwin, London, 1917), pp. 130-1.
6. 'Matriarchy', *Phoenix II*, p. 549.
7. Gibbs, *Since Then*, p. 371.
8. 'Matriarchy', *Phoenix II*, p. 549.
9. G. Evelyn Gates (ed.), *The Woman's Year Book 1923-1924* (Women Publishers, London, 1924), p. 308.
10. 'The Real Thing', *Phoenix*, p. 196.
11. Jane Lewis, 'Beyond Suffrage: English Feminism in the 1920s', *Maryland Historian*, vol. 6, no. 1 (1975), p. 4.
12. Gates, *The Woman's Year Book*, pp. 92-4.
13. Sheila Rowbotham, *A New World for Women* (Pluto Press, London, 1977), pp. 19-20.
14. *Woman's Leader*, 13 March 1925, p. 52.
15. Dora Russell, *Hypatia, or Woman and Knowledge* (Kegan Paul, Trench, Trubner, London, 1925), pp. 21 and 25.
16. Marie Stopes, *Marriage in My Time* (Rich and Cowan, London, 1935), p. 44.
17. Marie Stopes, *Married Love* (Putnam, London, 1918), p. xii.
18. Naomi Mitchison, *Comments on Birth Control* (Criterion Miscellany no. 12, Faber and Faber, London, 1930), p. 31.
19. Ibid., p. 6.
20. Muriel Box (ed.), *The Trial of Marie Stopes* (Femina Books, London, 1967), pp. 105-7.
21. J.B.S. Haldane, *Daedalus, or Science and the Future* (Kegan Paul, Trench, Trubner, London, 1924), pp. 64-8.
22. Vera Brittain, *Testament of Youth* (Victor Gollancz, London, 1933), p. 578.
23. Sheila Rowbotham, *Hidden from History* (Pluto Press, London, 1973), p. 124.
24. Q.D. Leavis, *Fiction and the Reading Public* (Chatto and Windus, London, 1932), p. 242.
25. Gibbs, *Since Then*, p. 379.
26. Ibid., p. 375.
27. Ibid., p. 382.
28. Ibid.
29. A contemporary of Lawrence and an early translator of Nietzsche,

Ludovici stressed the importance of the body and the instincts; claimed that, while men have both a sexual and a social role, women have only a sexual function; and emphasised the sexual potency of the working class. In addition to the works cited below, *A Defence of Aristocracy* (1915) is also of interest in its similarity to much of Lawrence's writing.

30. A.M. Ludovici, *Woman: A Vindication* (Constable, London, 1923), p. 278.

31. Ibid., p. 35.

32. A.M. Ludovici, *Lysistrata, or Woman's Future and Future Woman* (Kegan Paul, Trench, Trubner, London, 1925), p. 33.

33. Ibid., p. 76.

34. Ibid., p. 107.

35. A.M. Ludovici, *Man: An Indictment* (Constable, London, 1927), p. 114.

36. Ibid., p. 117.

37. Ibid., p. 358.

38. Brittain, *Testament of Youth*, p. 582.

39. 'WOMAN, German woman or American woman, or every other sort of woman, in the last war, was something frightening. As every *man* knows.' (*Studies in Classic American Literature*, p. 99.)

40. *Fantasia of the Unconscious*, p. 97.

41. Ibid., p. 99.

42. Ibid. The domestication of politics is satirised in several of the poems in the *Nettles* collection (1930), such as 'Change of Government', 'The British Workman and the Government' and 'Flapper Vote' (*Poems*, pp. 571-3).

43. *Fantasia of the Unconscious*, p. 135.

44. Letter to Lady Cynthia Asquith, 21 July 1915. *Letters*, vol. 2, p. 368.

45. *Fantasia of the Unconscious*, pp. 18, 102-3.

46. Ibid., p. 109.

47. Ibid., p. 100.

48. Ibid., p. 142.

49. Ibid., p. 95.

50. Ibid., p. 113.

51. *Phoenix II*, pp. 523-6.

52. *Fantasia of the Unconscious*, p. 189.

53. 'The Real Thing', *Phoenix*, p. 197.

54. *Studies in Classic American Literature*, p. 99.

55. Ibid., p. 100.

56. 'The Real Thing', *Phoenix*, p. 199.

57. *Aaron's Rod*, p. 110.

58. Ibid., p. 274.

59. Ibid., p. 340.

60. Ibid., pp. 122-3.

61. Ibid., p. 124.

62. Ibid., p. 192.

63. Ibid.

64. Ibid., p. 347.

65. Ibid., p. 346.

66. See Robert Darroch, *D.H. Lawrence in Australia* (Macmillan, Melbourne, 1981) for an account of the political movements depicted in *Kangaroo*.

67. *Kangaroo*, p. 108.

68. Ibid., p. 106.

69. Ibid., p. 219.

70. Ibid., p. 224.

71. Ibid., p. 125.

72. Ibid., p. 127.

73. Ibid., p. 132.
74. Ibid., p. 144.
75. Ibid., p. 120.
76. Ibid., p. 150.
77. Eliseo Vivas, *D.H. Lawrence: The Failure and the Triumph of Art* (Northwestern University Press, Evanston, 1960), p. 39.
78. *Kangaroo*, p. 195.
79. Ibid., pp. 40-1.
80. Ibid., pp. 195-6.
81. Begun 1923, put aside; worked on again, 1924-5; published 1926.
82. *The Plumed Serpent*, p. 133.
83. Ibid., p. 80.
84. Ibid., p. 176.
85. A complete reversal of the viewpoint set out in the *Study of Thomas Hardy*, written ten years previously.
86. *The Plumed Serpent*, p. 176.
87. Ibid., p. 162.
88. Ibid., p. 401.
89. Ibid., p. 402.
90. Ibid., p. 112.
91. Ibid., p. 420.
92. Ibid., p. 264.
93. Ibid., p. 365.
94. Ibid., p. 73.
95. Ibid., p. 153.
96. George H. Ford, *Double Measure* (Holt, Rinehart and Winston, New York, 1965), pp. 121-2.
97. *The Plumed Serpent*, p. 414.
98. Ibid., p. 415.
99. Ibid., p. 427.
100. Ibid., p. 462.
101. *St Mawr/The Virgin and the Gipsy*, p. 102.
102. Ibid., p. 164.
103. Ibid., pp. 57-8.
104. Ibid., p. 63.
105. Ibid., p. 144.
106. Ibid., p. 146.
107. Ibid., p. 127.
108. Ibid., p. 72.
109. It could be argued that in the early twenties Lawrence cut his links with England, and that it is tendentious to propose certain developments in English feminism and the position of women in England as one of the impetuses behind the novels of this period. Without underestimating Lawrence's genuine interest in the countries he visited on his 'savage pilgrimage', it seems to me that his overriding concern is always with the fate of western civilisation, and in particular with England. But, in any case, the developments in the position of women in this country were paralleled by those elsewhere. In the United States — probably the biggest single new influence on Lawrence's life and work in the twenties — the feminist movement had also become progressive and reformist. J. Stanley Lemons, *The Woman Citizen: Social Feminism in the 1920s* (University of Illinois Press, Urbana, 1973) provides ample evidence that the direction of the women's movement in the USA at this time was very close to that being taken in Great Britain, with similar results in social attitudes towards women.
110. John Edge, 'D.H. Lawrence and the Theme of Comradeship', *Southern Review*, vol. 9, no. 1 (1976), p. 43.

6 THE PHALLIC CONSCIOUSNESS

After the war it finally began to become acceptable to acknowledge, discuss and articulate female sexuality. But the results were perhaps not always those which the feminist movement might have hoped for. In 1917 Maude Royden, writing on 'modern love', had felt it necessary to point out that 'the abandonment of self-control in the intoxicating sense of being mastered' belonged to 'the pathological side of sex'.[1] Yet the female sexuality which now began to be portrayed both in 'scientific' studies and in literature was often founded on precisely this kind of masochism. Pioneers such as Freud or, on a more popular level, Marie Stopes, were at first castigated for daring to assert that female sexuality existed at all. But, this assertion once made, they challenged few of the basic assumptions about its nature. Stopes, for example, clung to contradictions which her biographer sees as contributing significantly to the popular success of *Married Love*; for while encouraging women to explore and assert their sexual needs, she none the less conceived of the sexual relationship in terms of 'the eminently desirable goddess pursued by the lustful hunter'.[2] Stopes could be said to have advocated the active acknowledgement and cultivation of an essentially passive female sexuality; a stance which was close to the popular distillation of Freudian theory. At least one historian of feminism has traced the decline of the movement in the late twenties and thirties to the direction taken by this post-war sexual revolution. According to Sheila Rowbotham, feminists had no political weapons with which to counter what she calls the cult of the 'Mean Man'.

> Instead of political opposition to feminism as a movement, the new defenders of patriarchy told women that their sexual needs could only be met by a man who humiliated them. The cult of the 'Mean Man' proved remarkably resilient and used as its stalking horse the rhetoric of sexual liberation . . . Women were told that feminism had made them unhappy, intellectual and frustrated. The 'Mean Man' brought sexual satisfaction — but at the price of submission.[3]

'Submission . . . masquerading as erotic liberation'[4] is the dominant motif of much popular literature in the twenties, a considerable amount of it written by women. Sheila Rowbotham ranks Lawrence along with the popular novelists in this respect, in what may seem to the literary critic to be a rather cavalier manner. But the affinities between them are significant, and it is possible to find, in the sensationalist romances of Ethel M. Dell and E.M. Hull and elsewhere, at least some sort of literary context for much of Lawrence's later work, the placing of which is a problem that perennially besets critics and literary historians. He shares with these writers certain themes and preoccupations which in both cases spring from an ambiguous response to the recent strides that had been taken towards the emancipation of women. In Lawrence's late work, and in the popular literature, the independence of women is the given starting-point, not the goal. The novels revolve around the question of what use women shall make of their freedom. The implied answer, in most cases, is that they will find fulfilment by voluntarily relinquishing it, and consigning themselves to the man who will satisfy their essentially masochistic sexual needs.

In *Fiction and the Reading Public*, first published in 1932, only two years after Lawrence's death, and still one of the best guides to the popular fiction of the twenties, Q.D. Leavis isolates a sentimental primitivism as one of the dominant themes in the popular novels of the period; a theme that was often explored through the conflict between a 'primitive' man and a 'civilised' woman. This conflict is well exemplified in the novel which has become a classic of the genre, Edith Maud Hull's *The Sheik*. Diana, the heroine of *The Sheik*, is, as her name suggests, a symbolic figure, a virgin huntress whose circumstances and fate are not merely individual, but representative of the situation of a whole generation. Like Lawrence's modern women — like Gudrun and Ursula in *Women in Love*, who have 'the remote, virgin look of modern girls, sisters of Artemis rather than of Hebe'[5] — she is ruled by the cold, chaste moon. Diana is twentieth-century woman — that is, she has been brought up (literally, in the novel) as a boy, to enjoy riding, hunting and adventure. She appears devoid of sexual feelings; as one admirer ruefully reflects, 'She's the coldest little fish in the world, without an idea in her head beyond sport and travel.'[6] Her upbringing has made Diana a feminist of sorts:

> I was brought up as a boy, my training was hard. Emotion and affection have been barred out of my life. I simply don't know what they mean. I don't want to know. I am very content with my life as it is. Marriage for a woman means the end of independence, that is, marriage with a man who is a man, in spite of all that the most modern woman may say. I have never obeyed anyone in my life;

I do not wish to try the experiment.[7]

A heroine of such naïvety is obviously heading for a fall, and the reader who knows or guesses the outcome of the story will relish the irony of Diana's innocent theorising:

> The idea of marriage — even in its highest form, based on mutual consideration and mutual forbearance — was repugnant to her . . . That women could submit to the degrading intimacy and fettered existence of married life filled her with scornful wonder. To be bound irrevocably to the will and pleasure of a man who would have the right to demand obedience in all that constituted marriage and the strength to enforce those claims revolted her.[8]

Against the advice of all her friends, Diana plans her most ambitious project, a trip through the North African desert accompanied only by native guides. She is captured by the Sheik, an Arab of unusually fastidious and Westernised personal habits, who subjects her to persistent sexual humiliation. After several attempts to escape, one of which results in her capture by a rival potentate of decidedly less refined habits, Diana realises that

> she had paid heavily for the determination to ignore the restrictions that her sex laid upon her . . . For the first time in her life she had had to obey. For the first time in her life she was of no account. For the first time she had been made conscious of the inferiority of her sex.[9]

Moreover, she is forced to acknowledge that she has actually fallen in love with her brutal captor:

> Quite suddenly she knew — knew that she loved him, that she had loved him a long time, even when she thought she hated him and when she had fled from him . . . He was a brute, but she loved him, loved him for his very brutality and superb animal strength.[10]

The Sheik postulates a female sexuality deeply rooted in passivity, negativity and masochism. Diana envisages 'an end of all individualism, a complete self-abnegation, an absolute surrender to his wishes, his moods and his temper'.[11]

The basic elements of this plot recur in many other popular novels of the period, especially those of Ethel M. Dell. The heroine has usually been brought up by a father or brother; this feature crops up so consistently that it must be seen as a convention for indicating that she has grown up in the 'man's world' of the twentieth century, and it also means that, since she has been deprived of models from whom to learn her feminine role, her subsequent initiation to this role is dramatic. The setting is the great outdoors, often the colonies or the Orient, or at the very least a farm; places where physical strength is still of some importance and where the effect of the physical differences between the sexes can be maximised. The argument from 'nature' and the belief that sexual roles are biologically rather than socially conditioned is particularly evident in the other classic of the genre, Edgar Rice Burroughs's *Tarzan of the Apes*. Tarzan grows up absolutely untouched by human social conditioning, raised by apes in the depths of the jungle, yet emerges complete with the views and behavioural patterns of the best sort of upper-class Englishman, including chivalry towards the weaker sex: 'He knew that she was created to be protected, and that he was created to protect her.'[12] The *status quo* is thus shown to be 'naturally' confirmed.

Lawrence's later fiction has several points of contact with these sensationalist romances. *The Plumed Serpent*, in particular, can be seen as Lawrence's attempt to write his own version of a novel in this clearly-defined genre – the exotic setting, the inscrutable, savage hero, and the initiation of an independent western woman into a passive and self-abnegating mode of female sexuality. *Lady Chatterley's Lover* is also constructed from the same elements, and both novels show traces of some of the most well-worn clichés of the popular literature. For example, the popular novelists were careful to give their savage heroes respectable backgrounds. Ahmed, the Sheik, turns out to be Viscount Caryll, educated in Paris and London, and an eminently eligible match; Tarzan is in fact the son of an English lord. In much the same way Cipriano, in *The Plumed Serpent*, has been educated at Oxford, and an acceptable pedigree is created for Mellors in *Lady Chatterley's Lover*; his dialect is partly an affectation, and he has an impeccable record as an army officer. There are remarkably similar scenes in *The Sheik* and *Lady Chatterley's Lover* where Diana and Connie respectively discover the reading habits of their lovers:

> She put the books back with a puzzled frown. She wished, with a feeling that she could not fathom, that they had been rather what she had imagined. The evidences of education and unlooked-for

tastes in the man they belonged to troubled her. It was an unexpected glimpse into the personality of the Arab who had captured her that was vaguely disquieting, for it suggested possibilities that would not have existed in a raw native, or one only superficially coated with a veneer of civilisation.[13]

She sighed, and got out of bed. The bare little room! Nothing in it at all but the small chest of drawers and the smallish bed. But the board floor was scrubbed clean. And in the corner by the window gable was a shelf with some books, and some from a circulating library. She looked. There were books about Bolshevist Russia, books of travel, a volume about the atom and the electron, another about the composition of the earth's core, and the causes of earthquakes: then a few novels: then three books on India. So! He was a reader after all.[14]

The themes of the 'cave-man' novels also recur in several of Lawrence's short stories. Dollie Urquhart, in 'The Princess', is a typical heroine. She has been brought up by her father and spent most of her life in travel. Like Diana in *The Sheik*, she is distant and independent:

The Princess learned her lesson early — the first lesson, of absolute reticence, the impossibility of intimacy with any other than her father . . . As a small child, something crystallized in her character, making her clear and finished, and as impervious as crystal.[15]

Like Diana again, she is unable to regard passionate relationships with anything except a kind of incredulous revulsion. 'The Princess she was, and the fairy from the North, and could never understand the volcanic phallic rage with which coarse people could turn on her in a paroxysm of hatred.'[16] And just as Diana was 'meant for a boy and changed at the last moment',[17] Dollie is 'not quite' a woman, but 'a changeling of some sort'.[18] The story develops along familiar lines, with an expedition (in this case into the Rocky Mountains) which isolates the virginal white woman with the savage man, in this case a Mexican guide. The conclusion of the tale is, however, purely Lawrentian in its account of a deathly kind of power struggle between a man and a woman who are attracted to each other. The battle of wills destroys both of them — Romero is shot, the Princess left 'a little mad'.[19] Lawrence's sympathy, however, seems to a large extent to be with the self-contained little Princess and, as in *St Mawr*, he avoids the clichéd ending to the story of the white woman and the savage man.

'Mother and Daughter' deals in a rather more comic vein with two women who obviously owe much to Mrs Witt and Lou in *St Mawr*. Virginia Bodoin (the name, like Diana's in *The Sheik*, is symbolic) has a career as 'head of a department in a certain government office'.[20] Mother and daughter scare away most of the men they encounter and live with each other in one of those love-hate relationships of dependency which Lawrence is so skilled at depicting. But Virginia's job does not go well:

> While she could work by quick intuition and without much responsibility, work thrilled her. But as soon as she had to get down to it, as they say, grip and slog and concentrate, in a really responsible position, it wore her out terribly. She had to do it all off her nerves. She hadn't the same sort of fighting power as a man. Where a man can summon his old Adam in him to fight through his work, a woman has to draw on her nerves, and on her nerves alone. For the old Eve in her will have nothing to do with such work. So that mental responsibility, mental concentration, mental slogging wear out a woman terribly, especially if she is head of a department, and not working *for* somebody.[21]

This passage echoes Lawrence's assertion in *Fantasia of the Unconscious* that 'the moment woman has got man's ideals and tricks drilled into her, the moment she is competent in the manly world — there's an end of it. She's had enough . . . She hates the thing she has embraced.'[22] A woman is as out of place in the man's world of the office as she is in the man's world of the jungle. But salvation for Virginia is forthcoming in the shape of 'the Armenian'.

> Mrs Bodoin, who barely tolerated him, and could never get his name which seemed to have a lot of bouyoums in it, called him either the Armenian or the Rahat Lakoum, after the name of the sweetmeat, or simply The Turkish Delight.[23]

Arnault the Armenian is a delightful parody of the Sheik type of hero, and from this point on the story rests delicately on a knife-edge between the serious and the comic.

> The Turkish Delight was sixty, grey-haired and fat. He had numerous grandchildren growing up in Bulgaria, but he was a widower. He had

his grey moustache cut like a brush, and glazed brown eyes over which hung heavy lids with white lashes.[24]

Yet this figure of fun is gradually established as a person of real solid power, and, against all the odds, the reader is persuaded that he might be a suitable mate for Virginia:

> True, he was fat, and he sat, with short thighs, like a toad, as if seated for a toad's eternity. His colour was of a dirty sort of paste, his black eyes were glazed under heavy lids . . .
> But his thick, fine white hair, which stood up on his head like a soft brush, was curiously virile. And his curious small hands, of the same soft dull paste, had a peculiar, fat, soft masculine breeding of their own. And his dull brown eye could glint with the subtlety of serpents, under the white brush of eyelash. He was tired, but he was not defeated . . . He was the father of sons, the head of a family, one of the heads of a defeated but indestructible tribe . . . His whole consciousness was patriarchal and tribal.[25]

Arnault's conquering of Virginia is both highly amusing and completely credible. The story is of interest, because although Lawrence professed contempt for *The Sheik* in 'Surgery for the Novel — Or A Bomb',[26] its basic concepts were extremely close to his heart. That is why, although the allusions in 'Mother and Daughter' depend for their comic effectiveness on the contrast between the dashing hero made famous by Valentino and the fat tradesman from the Levant, Lawrence and E.M. Hull are remarkably close in the message to women which is implied in their books: don't try to enter the man's world; acknowledge your destiny as the submissive mate of a strong man.

In the last chapter I demonstrated Lawrence's growing belief that a masculine renaissance was required in order to correct the subjugation and apathy into which men had fallen. At the same time he had formulated a mode of female sexuality, passionate yet passive, which would complement the new masculinity. But the heroes of his later novels and tales, although they share some of the characteristics of the 'mean men' portrayed in the popular literature, are at the same time more complex. One of Lawrence's foremost concerns in his later work is to extend the range of what is commonly understood as masculinity, and this is done primarily by developing the phallus into a symbol adequate to represent the full complexity of maleness. Lawrence comes to use the phallus as a symbol spanning every aspect —

religious, artistic, ethical – of his deepest convictions. There had always been phallic allusions in his other favourite emblems, the rainbow and the phoenix, and it is as if, in his final years, he traces these back to their ultimate source.

The appropriateness of the phallus for Lawrence's purposes is obvious. He was of course aware of its long and prestigious history as a religious symbol.[27] It embodies the idea of spontaneous life which was so important to him, since the capacity for erection is clearly dependent on something outside the range of the conscious will. The penis has a visible life of its own, and although the phallus is traditionally the image of an erect organ, it is not a static symbol, but carries with it the notion of change, of tumescence and detumescence. Lawrence invokes the detumescent as well as the erect penis, since to him the phallus is capable of symbolising the full range of values, including softness, tenderness and fragility. For, as many critics have noted, Lawrence's last years seem to herald a recoil from the obsession with power and a return to the values of love and gentleness.

> The hero is obsolete, and the leader of men is a back number. After all, at the back of the hero is the militant ideal: and the militant ideal, or the ideal militant, seems to me also a cold egg. We're sort of sick of all forms of militarism and militantism, and *Miles* is a name no more, for a man. On the whole I agree with you, the leader-cum-follower relationship is a bore. And the new relationship will be some sort of tenderness, sensitive, between men and men and men and women, and not the one up one down, lead on I follow, *ich dien* sort of business. So you see I'm becoming a lamb at last.[28]

At the same time as it is possible for the phallus to embody the 'feminine' qualities of tenderness and sensitivity, it remains, obviously, incontrovertibly masculine, and thereby allows Lawrence the opportunity to subsume the female principle into the male without, as it were, losing face. This has been noted by H.M. Daleski, who writes that 'Lawrence's invocation of the "phallic consciousness" betrays the infirmity of a divided self, for it is a subterfuge which enables him to identify himself with "female" qualities while preserving a "male" turn of phrase.'[29] Clearly, the notion of the phallus is crucial for Lawrence's late work. But discussion of this area is frequently hampered by the problematic nature of the word itself and its usage. A brief look at its history may therefore be in order.

Obviously 'phallus' is not a simple synonym for 'penis'. One suggested definition is 'the penis in its symbolic capacity',[30] which will serve as a starting-point. It originally denoted the image of an erect male organ carried in the festival of Dionysus and other ancient religious processions, and until the nineteenth century it seems to have been used in English almost exclusively with this relatively specialised meaning. In the nineteenth and early twentieth centuries there is evidence of another usage, not recorded in the *Oxford English Dictionary*, which is of some interest to literary critics. This is the use of 'phallic' and associated words to mean 'sexual' in a general (and usually disapproving) way, often with specific reference to the portrayal of erotic relationships in literature. In the *Latter-Day Pamphlets*, for example, Carlyle uses the term 'phallus-worship' more than once when attacking what he saw as the decadent literature of France. In 'Hudson's Statue', he talks of 'Literature of Desperation curiously conjoined with Phallus-Worship, too clearly heralding centuries of bottomless Anarchy',[31] and in 'Model Prisons' the phrase is used with reference to the works of Balzac and George Sand.

> If, moreover, I find the worship of Human Nobleness abolished in any country, and a *new* astonishing Phallus-Worship, with universal Balzac-Sand melodies and litanies in treble and in bass, established in its stead, what can I compute but that Nature, in horrible throes, will repugn against such substitution, — that, in short, the astonishing New Phallus-Worship, with its finer sensibilities of the heart, and 'great satisfying loves,' with its sacred kiss of peace for scoundrel and hero alike, with its all-embracing Brotherhood, and universal Sacrament of Divorce, will have to take itself away again![32]

There are interesting instances of this usage applied to Lawrence's own work. The *Daily News* review of *The Rainbow* called it a 'monotonous wilderness of phallicism',[33] while Ford Madox Ford, referring to an early draft of *The Trespasser*, said that it was 'much . . . more phallic than is the book as it stands'.[34] It is possible, then, that Lawrence deliberately embraced the vocabulary of phallicism with this kind of usage in mind, determined to shock his detractors with a novel, *Lady Chatterley's Lover*, that was truly phallic, a paean to the symbolic penis.

Since the turn of the century 'phallus' has been both more widely and more loosely used. It is now much more frequently employed in transferred and adjectival ways. Its greater currency is partly due to the influence of Freudian terminology; for although phrases such as 'phallic stage' remain technical terms, 'phallic symbol' has passed into common usage. The distinction between 'phallus' and 'penis' is also less sharp. (This point was debated in the correspondence columns of the *Times Literary Supplement* in 1972, after the publication of a review of Casanova's *History of My Life* under the title 'The Picaresque Phallus'.[35] One correspondent lamented the use of 'phallus' for 'penis', arguing that 'the distinction between a representation of the male organ and the organ itself is still a useful one';[36] another writer pointed out that modern 'sexologists' regularly use 'penis' to define 'the flaccid organ' and reserve 'phallus' for 'the erect organ'.[37])

The word does not, then, have a simple history. We may also note, as Ellen Moers does in *Literary Women*, that there is no female equivalent to 'phallus'.[38] To that extent, criticisms of Lawrence's usage such as that made by Eliseo Vivas, who demanded to know why a phallic marriage should not also be vaginal,[39] are misplaced. The corresponding adjective to 'vaginal' is not 'phallic' but 'penile'. As Moers points out, the female sexual organs have been worshipped as symbols of reproductive power to as great an extent as the male, but the symbolic word, at least in our culture, has been lost. Nor is there a neuter word which might cover the worship of any sexual symbol. Only 'phallus' has come down to us with something of the sacred and symbolic still clinging to it, reduced neither to an obscenity nor to a purely technical term. This does not exonerate Lawrence from his often consciously misogynist attitudes, but it does serve as a reminder that phallocentricity goes deeper than simple prejudice. With this in mind we may turn to the most common criticism of Lawrence's usage.

Lawrence has traditionally been accused by feminists of defining sexuality in male terms by using the word 'phallic' as a synonym for the word 'sexual'. Simone de Beauvoir writes: 'Lawrence believes passionately in the supremacy of the male. The very expression "phallic marriage", the equivalence he sets up between "sexual" and "phallic", constitute sufficient proof.'[40] Kate Millett makes the same point in her discussion of *Lady Chatterley's Lover*: 'In *Lady Chatterley*, as throughout his final period, Lawrence uses the words "sexual" and "phallic" interchangeably, so that the celebration of sexual passion for which the book is so renowned is largely a celebration of the penis of Oliver Mellors.'[41] The criticism is of course justified, and it has also been made by critics not specifically feminist in their approach, such as Vivas — although, as he points out, it is surprising how many writers on Lawrence pass over this idiosyncratic usage without comment. For example, in *Etruscan Places* Lawrence writes admiringly of the prominence given by the Etruscans to sexual symbolism — both male and female. 'The Etruscan consciousness,' he writes, 'was rooted quite blithely in these symbols, the phallus and the arx'[42] — the 'arx' being in his view a womb-symbol. But when Lawrence chooses a word to sum up the whole quality of Etruscan art and life — 'those easy natural proportions whose beauty one hardly notices, they come so naturally, physically'[43] — that word is 'phallic'. Again, in a letter to Mark Gertler, Lawrence writes: 'Wonder how your work goes. I've seen nothing for two years — but that nude you were doing in Sept. 1926 seemed to me to have some phallic glow too.'[44] A nude with the quality of 'phallic glow' might reasonably be supposed to be a painting of the male body, but although Gertler produced many fine female nudes during the twenties, he did not, as far as I have been able to discover, paint male nudes.[45] In Lawrence's usage, therefore, the female body is capable of possessing 'phallic glow'.

It is worth commenting on the fact that de Beauvoir and Millett, who criticise Lawrence for his phallocentric concept of sexuality, are amongst the many who have also levelled the same charge against Freud. I do not believe that Lawrence was in any way influenced by the prominence given to the phallus in Freudian theory — it is doubtful whether he ever read Freud with any degree of thoroughness, and in any case much of the relevant material was not published during his lifetime — but the parallels are interesting. There was of course a split quite early on in the psychoanalytic movement over the issue of Freud's phallocentricity — in particular his postulation of a 'phallic stage' in female development, and his organisation of a theory of female sexuality around the notorious concept of 'penis envy'. Karen Horney and Ernest Jones, amongst others, attempted to construct psychoanalytic theories of female sexuality that were not dependent on the phallus as an inescapable referent. This controversy is discussed, and the arguments of Freud's critics ably countered, by Juliet Mitchell in *Psychoanalysis and Feminism* (1974). By an ironic reversal, much of the recent theoretical work on female sexuality that has emerged from the contemporary women's movement has returned to the concept of the phallus as the ultimate determining factor in establishing the way that our categories of male and female are produced. This work draws heavily on the writings of Jacques Lacan, who accords the phallus, as 'unconscious representative',[46] a central place in his work. In his theory it is, in Mitchell's words, 'the very mark of human desire',[47] the term around which all our concepts of presence and absence, fullness and lack, and hence desire and sexual difference, come to be organised. Lacan's style endows the phallus with something of the *numen* that it has in Lawrence's work:

> The phallus is not a question of a form, or of an image, or of a phantasy, but rather of a signifier, the signifier of desire. In Greek antiquity the phallus is not represented by an organ but as an insignia; it is the ultimate significative object, which appears when all the veils are lifted.[48]

The phallus — rigorously stripped of any simple identification with the penis itself — becomes, in this branch of psychoanalytic theory, a neutral term, in relation to which both male and female sexuality evolve. 'Sexual difference *comes* to be represented . . . in relation to a common third term and that third term is the phallus.'[49] The attraction of this position for a certain school of feminist thought lies in its avoidance of the concept of an essential, pre-given femininity. On this level, the phallus has a less direct relationship than might be thought to masculinity and femininity, and even less to biological gender *per se*. It is merely the symbolic nexus of a multitude of possible relationships. Interestingly enough, Lawrence occasionally uses the symbol of the phallus in similar ways; as, for example, in his concept of it as the 'third term', and his determination to include within its range of values characteristics usually defined as feminine.

We may now look in more detail at Lawrence's usage. He of course used the word 'phallic' in its usual literal sense, speaking for example of 'phallic monuments',[50] or of things being 'phallic in shape'.[51] He also used it to mean 'functionally sexual', as in the passages on Tolstoy in 'The Novel', where he states that sex is more than just phallicism. It is clear that by this he means simple physical intercourse: 'For sex is so much more than phallic, and so much deeper than functional desire.'[52] Later, however, Lawrence came to use the term in a completely different sense. In a letter of 1928 he writes: 'I think even Rosanow [*sic*] was trying to express the phallic urge and consciousness, not merely the sexual.'[53] The meaning has completely swung around. 'Sexual' is no longer a larger, more inclusive term than 'phallic'; it is the latter which is now the wider term. It is true to say, therefore, that 'phallic' came to take the place of 'sexual' in Lawrence's vocabulary, but it would be misleading to assign too facile a significance to this usage. Lawrence felt the same desire to do away with the word 'sex' that so many people have felt about the word 'love'. The connotations which it bore among his contemporaries he found odious. Thus he writes of *Lady Chatterley's Lover* to Harriet Monroe: 'It is a nice and tender phallic novel − not a sex novel in the ordinary sense of the word.'[54] In Lawrence's usage, moreover, 'phallic' loses its association of thrusting aggressiveness and takes on feminine connotations: 'the phallic consciousness . . . is the source of all real beauty, and all real gentleness.'[55] It becomes linked with rhythmic cycles and with a rootedness in natural processes more usually assigned to female sexuality than to the sporadic and unpredictable manifestations of male desire. Lawrence declares, for example, that a 'phallic marriage' is 'linked up with the sun and the earth, the moon and the fixed stars and the planets, in the rhythm of days, in the rhythm of months, in the rhythm of quarters, of years, of decades and of centuries'.[56]

These concepts find expression in much of Lawrence's later fiction. The first full-length exploration of the theme is in *The Plumed Serpent*. The phallus is here the central symbol of a new kind of religion, rooted not in the spirit but in the body, and the cult of Quetzalcoatl is seen as restoring the true value of the phallus to a people who under Western, and particularly Christian, influence, have been denying its powers.

> When the snake of your body lifts its head, beware! It is I, Quetzalcoatl, rearing up in you . . . But men forgot me . . . When the snake of their body lifted its head, they said: This is the tame snake that does as we wish.[57]

Phallic power is most commonly conceived of in the novel as an unpredictable and violent force, like a tornado or a whirlwind:

> That pillar of cloud which swayed and swung, like a rearing serpent or a rising tree, till it swept the zenith, and all the earth below was dark and prone, and consummated . . . a whirlwind that rises suddenly in the twilight and raises a great pliant column, swaying and leaning with power, clear between heaven and earth.[58]

This rape of the earth by the phallic whirlwind reflects Lawrence's preoccupation, in this novel, with phallic *power*. It is the reverse side of the fruitful marriage between heaven and earth which is invoked in Kate's ritual mating with Cipriano. This is how Kate visualises the phallic landscape into which Cipriano transports her:

> She could see again the skies go dark, and the phallic mystery rearing itself like a whirling dark cloud, to the zenith, till it pierced the

sombre, twilit zenith; the old, supreme phallic mystery. And herself
in the everlasting twilight, a sky above where the sun ran smokily,
an earth below where the trees and creatures rose up in blackness,
and man strode along naked, dark, half-visible, and suddenly whirled
in supreme power, towering like a dark whirlwind column, whirling
to pierce the very zenith.[59]

It is a sinister vision, and seems to reflect Lawrence's ambiguity towards
the concept of power which he is exploring. In the novel, however, he
does develop another theme which is not, at this stage, specifically
related to the phallus, but which I have indicated as important in the
growth of his ideas. This is the notion that tenderness, grace, beauty,
humility and so on are masculine attributes; and, moreover, intrinsic
attributes, rather than essentially feminine qualities which in an ideal
man might be grafted onto his masculinity. Kate is aware, in the
Mexican men, of 'passionate male tenderness',[60] 'dark, physical tenderness',[61] 'the stillness, the humility and the pathos of grace . . . something very beautiful and truly male, and very hard to find in a civilized
white man'.[62] In the novel Lawrence consistently uses words such as
'soft', 'full', 'delicate', 'vulnerable' and 'pure' to describe men, balancing the other images of violence and power more traditionally associated with masculinity.

In *The Plumed Serpent* the word 'phallus' is used over and over
again, but no distinction between the phallus and the penis is made, and
indeed, the latter word is never used. The novel concerns itself with the
phallus in its traditional role as a religious symbol, which has the effect
of making it seem a much less outrageous work than *Lady Chatterley's
Lover*, where there is insistence on the physical organ as well as on the
symbol. In *The First Lady Chatterley* religious symbolism recurs, but is
associated much more closely with the penis itself:

> She thought of the naked man, the passion and the mystery of him;
> the mystery of the penis! And she knew, as every woman knows,
> that the penis is the column of blood, the living fountain of fullness
> in life . . . Whatever else it is, it is the river of the only God we can
> be sure about, the blood. 'There is a fountain filled with blood,' said
> the hymn. And it is eternally true.[63]

Lawrence was not of course unaware of the semantic distinction:
'And the *symbol* of the rush of the living blood is the phallus, and the
penis is the fountain of life filled with blood.'[64] But his insistence, at

times, on blurring it can lead to passages such as the following, which are very difficult to take seriously and which critics such as Kate Millett have quite rightly ridiculed: 'It is the penis which connects us sensually with the planets. But for the penis we should never know the loveliness of Sirius or the categorical difference between a pomegranate and an india-rubber ball.'[65]

In *John Thomas and Lady Jane*, the second of the three versions of the novel, the distinction between phallus and penis is explored rather more thoughtfully. The ability to realise the symbolic dimension of the male organ, to possess not merely a penis but a phallus, becomes the necessary preliminary to participation in the new masculinism which Lawrence is advocating.

> To most men, the penis was merely a member, at the disposal of the personality. Most men merely used their penis as they use their fingers, for some personal purpose of their own. But in a true man, the penis has a life of its own, and is the second man within the man. It is prior to the personality. And the personality must yield before the priority and the mysterious root-knowledge of the penis, or the phallus. For this is the difference between the two: the penis is a mere member of the physiological body. But the phallus, in the old sense, has roots, the deepest roots of all, in the soul and the greater consciousness of man, and it is through the phallic roots that inspiration enters the soul.[66]

Lawrence also develops, in this version of the novel, the concept of the phallus as something which links, and thereby comes to include in itself, both male and female qualities. For example, the symbolic dimension of the organ, once established, need not be limited to its erect, tumescent form; the phallus 'so little now, like a bud, and innocent'[67] is equally significant. It also comes to represent the third term in the relationship between a man and a woman, symbolising their union and belonging not just to one of them, but at once to both and to neither.

> Vaguely, she realised for the first time in her life what the phallus meant, and her heart seemed to enter a new, wide world. Between the two hesitating, baffled creatures, himself and her, she had seen the third creature, erect, alert, overweening, utterly unhesitating, stand there in a queer new assertion, rising from the roots of his body. It was like some primitive, grotesque god: but alive, and

unspeakably vivid, alert with its own weird life, apart from both their personalities.[68]

Male and female together form the perfect circle of the 'phallic body',[69] a notion which Lawrence expanded in *A Propos of Lady Chatterley's Lover*:

> Two rivers of blood, are man and wife, two distinct eternal streams, that have the power of touching and communing and so renewing, making new one another, without any breaking of the subtle confines, any confusing or commingling. And the phallus is the connecting-link between the two rivers, that establishes the two streams in a oneness, and gives out of their duality a single circuit, forever.[70]

In the final version of the novel, some of this is lost at the expense of a considerable emphasis on the 'feminine' aspects of the phallus. In his descriptions of the lovemaking of Connie and Mellors, Lawrence is at pains to stress Connie's newly discovered appreciation of the penis as a thing capable of delicacy and gentleness as well as power.

> Now all her body clung with tender love to the unknown man, and blindly to the wilting penis, as it so tenderly, frailly, unknowingly withdrew, after the fierce thrust of its potency. As it drew out and left her body, she gave an unconscious cry of pure loss ... And only now she became aware of the small, bud-like reticence and tenderness of the penis, and a little cry of wonder and poignancy escaped her again, her woman's heart crying out over the tender frailty of that which had been the power.[71]

Although the theoretical statements on the phallus as the 'third term' disappear in the final version (to reappear as a sort of gloss on the novel in *A Propos of Lady Chatterley's Lover*), the notion is to some extent implicit in Connie's phallic paeans:

> 'And now he's tiny, and soft like a little bud of life!' she said, taking the soft small penis in her hand. 'Isn't he somehow lovely! so on his own, so strange! And so innocent! ... He's mine too. He's not only yours.'[72]

The process of feminising the phallus also includes establishing its association with a mode of sexuality more usually considered feminine.

The Lawrentian phallus gives birth to the cosmos with all the broodiness of a mother hen:

> She quivered again at the potent inexorable entry inside her, so strange and terrible. It might come with the thrust of a sword in her softly-opened body, and that would be death. She clung in a sudden anguish of terror. But it came with a strange slow thrust of peace, the dark thrust of peace and a ponderous, primordial tenderness, such as made the world in the beginning.[73]

In the first half of 1928 Lawrence wrote a whole series of letters to friends and acquaintances promoting his newly-finished novel, repeatedly describing it as 'phallic' and emphasising that it was primarily about 'tenderness'.[74] To this extent, of course, Lawrence's last novel does represent a return to the 'feminine' values which he had advocated before the war. By a neat reversal these values are now 'masculine', leaving his women characters the choice of either identifying with the new 'feminine' values of cerebration, will, technology and so on, or of becoming disciples of the new masculinism. This is the situation that Connie faces in what is really a Hobson's choice between Clifford and Mellors.

It is also a choice between what Lawrence saw as two distinct modes of female sexuality. The exaltation of the phallus in his work is accompanied by loathing of the clitoris, its female equivalent. Lawrence makes a categoric distinction between clitoral and vaginal orgasm, steering his female characters away from the former and towards the latter. In the notorious passage in *The Plumed Serpent* in which Kate renounces 'the seething, frictional, ecstatic Aphrodite of the foam', it is not orgasm itself which Cipriano denies her, as most critics have inferred, but clitoral sensation: the 'beak-like friction', the 'seething electric female ecstasy, which knows such spasms of delirium'.[75] Kate has always understood this to be what constitutes her sexual satisfaction, but it is supplanted by passive vaginal orgasm described in terms which have shaped a whole modern mythology of female sexuality: 'And he . . . would bring her back to the new, soft, heavy, hot flow, when she was like a fountain gushing noiseless and with urgent softness from the volcanic deeps.'[76] The same process is traced in *Lady Chatterley's Lover*. With Michaelis, Connie enjoys active, clitoral orgasm — a fact which he later uses to taunt her, in an episode which distorts for ever her concept of her own sexuality. Mellors reveals to her a similar disgust at the active sexuality of his former wife:

> By God, you think a woman's soft down there, like a fig. But I tell you the old rampers have beaks between their legs, and they tear at you with it till you're sick . . . She had to work the thing herself, grind her own coffee. And it came back on her like a raving necessity, she had to let herself go, and tear, tear, tear, as if she had no sensation in her except in the top of her beak, the very outside top tip, that rubbed and tore. That's how old whores used to be, so men used to say.[77]

This is of course related to a hazard inherent in the very process of symbolising the penis as the phallus, for symbolisation can easily slide into reification, with the result that the phallus becomes merely an object that the woman can use for her own sexual gratification. This is Connie's instinctive reaction at the beginning of her affair with Mellors, when she fears that the strength of her feelings for him will leave her 'effaced, a slave, like a savage woman':[78]

> Ah yes, to be passionate like a Bacchante, like a Bacchanal fleeing through the woods, to call on Iacchos, the bright phallos that had no independent personality behind it, but was pure god-servant to the woman! The man, the individual, let him dare not intrude. He was but a temple-servant, the bearer and keeper of the bright phallos, her own.
>
> So, in the flux of new awakening, the old hard passion flamed in her for a time, and the man dwindled to a contemptible object, the mere phallos-bearer, to be torn to pieces when his service was performed.[79]

But the orgasms which Connie comes to experience with Mellors are passive. 'She could no longer harden and grip for her own satisfaction upon him. She could only wait.'[80] The adjectives for this new form of sexuality are 'helpless', 'soft', 'melting', 'unconscious' and 'rhythmic', the images those of liquid rippling – oceans, tides, whirlpools, bells.

Along with this aversion to the clitoris goes a disgust with menstruation. The Lawrentian insistence on the blood refers, never to the monthly flow, but always to the blood which swells the erect penis. 'The penis is the column of blood, the living fountain of fullness of life. From the strange rising and surging of the blood all life rushes into being.'[81] In a typical conflation of Christianity and femininity, Lawrence declares that both menstrual blood and the blood shed by Christ on the cross (itself 'the symbol of the murdered phallus')[82] are unclean compared to the blood that transforms penis into phallus. 'And it is not the dead, spilled blood which will wash away all sin, but the living rush of the ever new blood ever renewed. Dead blood can but stink at last.'[83]

An extreme instance of revulsion towards female sexuality is portrayed in Parkin's case-history in *John Thomas and Lady Jane*. A traumatic experience as a child leaves the gamekeeper with an aversion to female pubic hair, and he is unable to make love to his wife until he has shaved her — an operation with strong overtones of female castration.[84] This aversion is of course counterbalanced by episodes elsewhere in the novel and can hardly be said to represent Lawrence's own feelings, but it is significantly linked with Bertha's sexual assertiveness: 'An' when she did sleep with me, she wanted it all her own way, I was nowhere: as if she was the man, an' me the woman.'[85]

The reversal of sexual roles implied in Bertha's behaviour is one symptom of a general sexual *malaise* which also manifests itself in Mrs Bolton's perverted maternal relationship with Clifford and in the Wragby drawing-room talk. It is a *malaise* which Connie herself has not escaped, since the novel carefully establishes her pedigree as a modern woman, and which has also claimed Mellors as its victim. Thus, although Lawrence's last novel is frequently seen as a pastoral, a timeless exploration of sexual passion determined more by myth than by history, the historical context is crucial. The solution for both Connie and Mellors lies in the values now symbolised by the phallus, for 'it's because th' men *aren't* men, that th' women have to be.'[86]

Notes

1. A Maude Royden, 'Modern Love' in Victor Gollancz (ed.), *The Making of Women: Oxford Essays in Feminism* (Allen and Unwin, London, 1917), p. 61.
2. Ruth Hall, *Marie Stopes* (André Deutsch, London, 1977), p. 132.
3. Sheila Rowbotham, *Hidden from History* (Pluto Press, London, 1973), p. 126.
4. John Edge, 'D.H. Lawrence and the Theme of Comradeship', *Southern Review*, vol. 9, no. 1 (1976), p. 49.
5. *Women in Love*, p. 54.
6. E.M. Hull, *The Sheik* (Eveleigh Nash, London, 1919), pp. 6-7.
7. Ibid., pp. 14-15.
8. Ibid., p. 38.
9. Ibid., pp. 89 and 92.
10. Ibid., p. 132.
11. Ibid., p. 162.
12. Edgar Rice Burroughs, *Tarzan of the Apes* (Methuen, London, 1917), p. 147.

13. Hull, *The Sheik*, pp. 69-70.
14. *Lady Chatterley's Lover*, pp. 221-2.
15. *The Princess and Other Stories*, p. 26.
16. Ibid., p. 28.
17. Hull, *The Sheik*, p. 6.
18. *The Princess and Other Stories*, p. 36.
19. Ibid., p. 72.
20. Ibid., p. 221.
21. Ibid., pp. 232-3.
22. *Fantasia of the Unconscious*, p. 189.
23. *The Princess and Other Stories*, p. 237.
24. Ibid., p. 289.
25. Ibid., pp. 239-40.
26. 'The mass of the populace "find themselves" in the popular novels. But nowadays it's a funny sort of self they find. A Sheik with a whip up his sleeve, and a heroine with weals on her back, but adored in the end, adored, the whip out of sight, but the weals still faintly visible.' (*Phoenix*, p. 519.)
27. *Etruscan Places*, passim.
28. Letter to Witter Bynner, 13 March 1928. *Collected Letters*, p. 1045.
29. H.M. Daleski, *The Forked Flame* (Faber and Faber, London, 1965), p. 260.
30. Thorkil Vanggaard, *Phallós: A Symbol and its History in the Male World* (Jonathan Cape, London, 1972), p. 11.
31. Thomas Carlyle, 'Hudson's Statue', *Latter-Day Pamphlets* (Chapman and Hall, London, 1850), p. 43.
32. Carlyle, 'Model Prisons', ibid., p. 41.
33. Robert Lynd, 'The Downfall', *Daily News and Leader*, 5 October 1915, p. 6.
34. Ford Madox Ford, *Mightier than the Sword* (Allen and Unwin, London, 1938), p. 121.
35. *Times Literary Supplement*, 1 September 1972, pp. 1009-11.
36. Ibid., 15 September 1972, p. 1060.
37. Ibid., 29 September 1972, p. 1156.
38. Ellen Moers, *Literary Women* (W.H. Allen, London, 1977), pp. 256-7.
39. Eliseo Vivas, *D.H. Lawrence: The Failure and the Triumph of Art* (Northwestern University Press, Evanston, 1960), p. 268.
40. Simone de Beauvoir, *The Second Sex*, tr. H.M. Parshley (Jonathan Cape, London, 1953), pp. 228-9.
41. Kate Millett, *Sexual Politics* (Hart-Davis, London, 1971), p. 238.
42. *Mornings in Mexico* and *Etruscan Places*, p. 110.
43. Ibid., pp. 106-7.
44. Letter to Mark Gertler, 24 May 1928. *Collected Letters*, p. 1062.
45. See 'A Catalogue of the Work of Mark Gertler' in John Woodeson, *Mark Gertler: Biography of a Painter, 1891-1939* (Sidgwick and Jackson, London, 1972), pp. 357-91).
46. Parveen Adams, 'Representation and Sexuality, *m/f*, no. 1 (1978), p. 67.
47. Juliet Mitchell, *Psychoanalysis and Feminism* (Allen Lane, London, 1974), p. 395.
48. Jacques Lacan, *The Language of the Self: The Function of Language in Psychoanalysis*, tr. A. Wilden (Johns Hopkins Press, Baltimore, 1968), p. 187.
49. Adams, 'Representation and Sexuality', p. 66.
50. Letter to Richard Aldington, 18 April 1926. *Collected Letters*, p. 901.
51. Letter to Dorothy Brett, 20 January 1917. Ibid., p. 960.
52. *Phoenix II*, p. 426.
53. Letter to Max Mohr, 22 March 1928. *Collected Letters*, p. 1048. For

Rozanov's possible influence on Lawrence's theory of phallicism see George J. Zytaruk, 'The Phallic Vision: D.H. Lawrence and V.V. Rozanov', *Comparative Literature Studies*, vol. 4, no. 3 (1967), pp. 283-9.

54. Letter to Harriet Monroe, 15 March 1928. *Collected Letters*, p. 1046.
55. Ibid.
56. *À Propos of Lady Chatterley's Lover*, p. 111. I have silently corrected an error in the Penguin text which prints 'plants' for 'planets'.
57. *The Plumed Serpent*, pp. 132-3.
58. Ibid., pp. 324-5.
59. Ibid., p. 324.
60. Ibid., p. 78.
61. Ibid., p. 130.
62. Ibid., p. 116.
63. *The First Lady Chatterley*, p. 156.
64. Ibid., my emphasis.
65. Ibid.
66. *John Thomas and Lady Jane*, p. 238.
67. Ibid., p. 242.
68. Ibid., pp. 237-8.
69. Ibid., p. 239. It could of course be argued that the concept of the phallus as something 'with a life of its own' reflects a reluctance on the part of men to take responsibility for their own sexuality.
70. *À Propos of Lady Chatterley's Lover*, p. 112.
71. *Lady Chatterley's Lover*, pp. 181-2.
72. Ibid., p. 219.
73. Ibid., p. 181.
74. *Collected Letters*, pp. 1042-64, *passim*.
75. *The Plumed Serpent*, p. 439.
76. Ibid.
77. *Lady Chatterley's Lover*, pp. 210-11.
78. Ibid., p. 141.
79. Ibid.
80. Ibid., pp. 138-9.
81. *The First Lady Chatterley*, p. 156.
82. Ibid., p. 157.
83. Ibid., p. 156.
84. The similarities to the case of Ruskin are obvious. Ruskin's wife Effie wrote that the reason for the non-consummation of their marriage was 'that he had imagined women were quite different to what he saw I was . . . he did not make me his Wife . . . because he was disgusted with my person the first evening'. (William James, *The Order of Release: The Story of John Ruskin, Effie Gray and John Everett Millais* (John Murray, London, 1947), p. 221.) That Lawrence knew something of Ruskin's biography is evident from *Fantasia of the Unconscious*, p. 121.
85. *John Thomas and Lady Jane*, p. 231.
86. *Lady Chatterley's Lover*, p. 229.

7 A LITERARY TRESPASSER

> I think the only re-sourcing of art, re-vivifying it, is to make it more the joint work of man and woman. *D.H. Lawrence*[1]

> Plagiarisms begin at home. *Zelda Fitzgerald*[2]

An aspect of D.H. Lawrence's work which has generally passed unremarked by critics is the extent to which he used women as actual or potential collaborators, and women's writing as source material. For example, *The Boy in the Bush*, which was published under the joint authorship of Lawrence and Mollie Skinner, has been largely ignored in critical studies.[3] Again, it is now well known that *The Trespasser* was based upon an autobiographical prose-poem of Helen Corke's, but when this fact is mentioned in passing it is usually to imply that any faults in the novel result from Lawrence's use of an 'inferior' writer's work as his starting-point. Little attempt has been made to examine the implications of this curious and significant part of Lawrence's technique, yet, from the involvement of Jessie Chambers and Louie Burrows in his earliest literary ventures, through to the novels that were planned in conjunction with Mollie Skinner, Mabel Dodge Luhan and Catherine Carswell in the 1920s, collaboration with women and reliance on their writing remained a constant feature of his method.

When commentators *have* remarked upon this fact, they have played down its significance. Thus, Harry T. Moore, writing of the 'Miriam Papers' (notes by Jessie Chambers which formed the basis for scenes in *Sons and Lovers*), warns against assuming that Jessie was in any real sense a collaborator in the novel, and merely adds:

> Although Lawrence had from the feminine elements in his own nature a remarkable intuitive understanding of women, he would sometimes ask the women he knew to write down what they had felt or possibly would feel in certain situations: in this way various women provided him with some of his 'sources'.[4]

But Lawrence not only solicited notes and reminiscences from Jessie, Frieda, Mabel Dodge Luhan and others — in itself a fairly unusual procedure — he also took over women's manuscripts and rewrote them, as in the cases of Helen Corke and Mollie Skinner, and once or twice made attempts at a genuine collaboration. It is of course a truism that most novelists draw to some extent on the circumstances and experiences of those close to them, as well as on their own experiences, for the substance of their art. In adopting the exterior details of Louie Burrows's home and family background for the character of Ursula in *The Rainbow*, for instance, Lawrence was not doing anything very unusual. A novelist may also make use of others to check details or provide facts; so that we find, for example, Lawrence asking Jessie 'to take a tram ride out to Basford and bring him word what the registry office looked like'[5] when he was writing an early version of *The White Peacock*. But this sort of incidental reliance on information furnished willingly or unwittingly by his women acquaintances is of a different order from his more extensive rewriting of women's experience. Nor can Lawrence's practice be discussed in terms of simple plagiarism or the influence of one literary work upon another — what are involved are those private processes of collaboration and revision which rarely receive attention.

Lawrence seems to have thought it crucial that female experience should find expression in the novel, and he never gives the impression of consciously wishing to repress women's writing. On the contrary, the evidence shows that he gave forceful encouragement to the women he knew in their own literary work: one has only to look at his letters to Catherine Carswell. He was frequently annoyed when they wouldn't, or couldn't, write as effortlessly and copiously as he himself did. He never expected the women he knew to take the role of amanuensis (although some of them volunteered for the part), and he appears to have been ready to take women's criticism of his own work seriously. Yet Lawrence's encouragement and his expectation of high standards could shade off into anger and impatience when these standards were not met — or, one suspects, when the writer in question had standards of her own. At such times Lawrence's reaction was usually that *he* could do better. He was only intermittently aware of the special problems faced by women writers. He was never interested in detailed, patient revision, either of his own work or of other people's. His preferred method of revising his own novels was to start writing them out again from the beginning, and he often gave others' writing the same treatment. In this respect the genesis of the poem 'Coldness in Love'[6] is interesting. On one occasion Helen Corke showed Lawrence a poem she had written called 'Fantasy', about a trip they had made together to the coast.[7] Lawrence promptly produced his own poem, based on the same situation, taking Helen's theme and recasting it to his own satisfaction. The final printed version could be in the voice of a man or a woman, but in fact the emotions are Helen's, as her autobiography reveals, although anyone reading the poem without a knowledge of its background would assume them to be Lawrence's. Lawrence commented to her, 'I always feel, when you give me an idea, how much better I could work it out myself!'[8] – an appropriate epigraph to any discussion of Lawrence's attitude towards women's articulation of their own experience in literary form.

It does not appear that Lawrence's collaborating instincts extended to his male friends to the same degree. He worked with his friend S.S. Koteliansky on translations from Russian; Lawrence would completely rewrite Koteliansky's basic English version, polishing up the style as he went along.[9] But he never involved other men in the process of composition in the way he did women. The traditional explanation has been that Lawrence, being a man, could draw the feelings and reactions of his male characters from his own experience, while with female characters he needed to be sure that he had 'got it right'. But such an explanation presupposes areas of sexually-defined experience to which anyone of the appropriate gender has access; and there is also a historical dimension to the question which must be borne in mind.

It is now generally acknowledged that the history of the novel as a literary form is in many ways closely bound up with the history of women. To an extent which has no real parallel in other genres, women have been conspicuous as the authors, the readers and the subject matter of novels. Women writers have used the novel more than any other literary form, and recent feminist criticism has quite rightly drawn attention to their achievements. But we must also take into account the fact that male novelists have to an unusual degree organised their works specifically around women's experience.

A significant number of early English novels are books by men which purport in some way to be first-hand accounts of women's lives. In Defoe's *Moll Flanders* (1722), for example, Moll appears to be telling her own story in the first person, and Defoe claims to have merely edited it 'from her own memorandums'. In the Preface he talks of the difficulties he has had in making Moll's account fit for publication:

It is true, that the original of this Story is put into new Words, and the Stile of the famous Lady we here speak of, is a little alter'd, particularly she is made to tell her own Tale in modester Words than she told it at first; the Copy which came first to Hand, having been written in Language more like one still in *Newgate* than one grown Penitent and Humble, as she afterwards pretends to be.

The Pen employ'd in finishing her Story, and making it what you see it to be, has had not little Difficulty to put it into a Dress fit to be seen, and to make it speak Language fit to be read: When a Woman debauch'd from her Youth, nay, even being the Off-spring of Debauchery and Vice, comes to give an Account of all her vicious Practises, and even to descend to the particular Occasions and Circumstances, by which she first became wicked, and of all the progressions of Crime, which she run through in Threescore Years, an Author must be hard put to it to wrap it up so clean, as not to give room, especially for vicious Readers, to turn it to his Disadvantage.[10]

We may see here the seeds of the concept of a male *editing* of women's experience which has been a crucial factor in the development of the novel. Defoe claims not only to be polishing, but also to be censoring, a woman's account of her own life.

In Samuel Richardson's tremendously influential novels, *Pamela* (1740) and *Clarissa Harlowe* (1747-8), another variety of first-person narrative, the letter, is used to give the reader the impression that he or she has a privileged and unmediated access to the most intimate thoughts and experiences of the heroine. Richardson was widely praised for his delineation of female experience, and while this was partly a matter of sensibility, it was also based on some solid research. He had a large circle of women friends with whom he kept up a steady correspondence about his writing, soliciting and incorporating their suggestions, and in turn encouraging them in their own literary work. This is a pattern which crops up with significant frequency in the lives of male novelists. These members of Richardson's circle played a particularly important part in the composition of Richardson's third novel, also in epistolary form, *Sir Charles Grandison*; they contributed whole scenes and one of them completely revised the manuscript. Richardson went so far as to plan a sequel to *Sir Charles Grandison* which was to be wholly a collaborative effort, consisting entirely of letters contributed by his women friends, but this project failed to materialise.[11]

As narrative technique became more sophisticated it no longer became necessary for the novelist to insist on the psychological veracity of his fiction by casting it in autobiographical or epistolary form, but the part played by female experience as subject matter continued to be important as the novel developed. The orientation of the male novelist of Lawrence's period is complex because, as Carolyn Heilbrun has noted, 'for a period of nearly fifty years such major writers as Ibsen, James, Shaw, Lawrence, Forster were to find that, at the height of their powers, it was a woman hero who best met the requirements of their imaginations'.[12] Heilbrun defines the 'woman hero' as specifically the creation of male writers who found in the predicament of modern woman, in 'the peculiar tension that exists between her apparent freedom and her actual relegation to a constrained destiny',[13] a metaphor for a more general existential dilemma; the problems that the modern novelist is dealing with appear in a heightened form, or at least a form more appropriate for examination in art, in women's experience. In addition, the trend of the modern novel has been towards a rendering of inner psychological states rather than of action, of exploring unconscious rather than conscious processes, and our sexual mythology commonly designates these areas of experience 'feminine'. For a writer as hostile as Lawrence was to most of the conventionally masculine values of logic, abstraction and technology, the mythology of femininity as something based on intuition, unconsciousness and emotion would have made the choice of a 'woman hero', or at least the choice to write about female experience, almost irresistible.

The issue of the male novelist's rendering of female experience must also take into account what Rosalind Miles has described as 'the assumption that literary creation is itself a masculine act, a process of exploring and mastering the feminine, unconscious mass of life and material'.[14] Indeed, Lawrence can frequently give the impression that he considered the evocation of feminine reality too momentous and urgent a task to be left to women. Kate Millett has of course made the point that by expressing his 'message' – particularly the notion of female submissiveness – through women characters, Lawrence is being a particularly subtle propagandist.[15] But it seems to be the pervasive concept of femininity as 'raw material' and masculinity as 'shaping force' which underlies his use of women's writing.

Co-operation with women is present from the very inception of Lawrence's writing career. The early letters to Louie Burrows show that he thought of her, Jessie Chambers and himself as all in some sense budding young writers.

> I write to you as a would-be aspirant after literature, for I know you are such . . . I think you will do well. You are brighter than Jessie, more readable, but you are not so powerful. You will doubtless succeed far better than I who am so wilful . . . Let me see what you

do — I am all interest.[16]

The same letter contains a rather schoolmasterly criticism of a piece of Louie's writing:

> Like most girl writers you are wordy. I have read nearly all your letters to J[essie], so I do not judge only from this composition. Again and again you put in interesting adjectives and little phrases which make the piece loose, and sap its vigour. Do be careful of your adjectives — do try and be terse, there is so much more force in a rapid style that will not be hampered by superfluous details.[17]

Lawrence also invites Louie's comments on his own work — 'Write me your opinions and criticisms — your advice if you like — I shall like it'[18] — although we do not know whether she responded to the challenge.

Throughout the years 1906-8 the letters to Louie contain frequent references to her writing (none of which is now extant), encouraging her in the task of revising and commiserating when she started work as a teacher and found she had less time. But Lawrence gradually seems to assume an air of superiority in this literary friendship. In 1907 three short stories were submitted for a Christmas competition in the *Nottinghamshire Guardian*. One bore the name of D.H. Lawrence, one that of Jessie Chambers, and the third that of Louie Burrows. In fact all three ('Legend', later given the title 'A Fragment of Stained Glass', 'A Prelude', and 'The White Stocking') were by Lawrence; he had asked Jessie and Louie to submit one each under their names as each entrant was allowed only one attempt. ('A Prelude' won the competition and appeared under Jessie's name in the *Guardian* of 7 December 1907.) Lawrence had allowed Louie to revise 'The White Stocking' in her own style before submitting it, but the beginnings of a more patronising attitude are evident. By 1909 Lawrence seems to have assumed the role of Louie's editor and agent:

> I am glad you are writing stories. I can't do 'em myself. Send me them, please, and I'll see if I can put a bit of surface on them and publish them for you. We'll collaborate, shall we? — I'm sure we should do well. At any rate send me the tales at once, and I'll send em to the publisher some time or other in your name.[19]

Lawrence several times mentions revising Louie's writing for her. In returning one piece to her, he warns, 'Here is your tale — you will not like it';[20] another time he asks her to send him 'any more of yours you want to see "slaughtered" '.[21] The short story 'Goose Fair' seems to have been the result of some sort of genuine collaboration. Lawrence originally submitted it to a press agency under a fictitious name that must have been a hybrid of his own and Louie's. 'The nom de guerre, as you will see, is a happy mixture of you and me: you are the body, I the head. Qu'en dites vous? I believe you are utterly unrecognisable under my figurehead.'[22] One wonders if it was simply chance that led Lawrence to designate Louie the 'body' and himself the 'head' in their collaborative pseudonym, and whether his assurance to her that she is now 'unrecognisable' is not indicative of something more sinister than a possible desire on her part to remain anonymous. For the press agency plan fell through, and when the story was finally published in *The English Review* for February 1910 it appeared under Lawrence's name alone — although he insisted to Louie that it was 'as much your child as mine', and split the fee he received for its publication with her in acknowledgement of this.[23] After Lawrence became engaged to Louie in December 1910 her involvement in his literary work lessened. By this time Lawrence was writing *Paul Morel*, later to become *Sons and Lovers*, and his literary collaborator was Jessie Chambers. But with Louie he established a pattern that was to recur several times with other women.

Lawrence's relationship with Jessie Chambers was crucial not only in his psychological but also in his literary development. This latter aspect has only recently begun to be fully acknowledged by critics. During one of their many quarrels, Lawrence tried to persuade Jessie that he should be allowed to marry a woman who would be a purely physical wife to him, while continuing his intellectual relationship with her. Jessie replied that she did not want a part-share in someone else's husband, although she was reluctant to 'refuse the co-operation that he said was essential to his work'. She asked him why, if he did not love her, he did not simply end their relationship. His answer, she says, 'came with shattering sincerity: "Because you are necessary to me." '[24] This necessity which Jessie filled in Lawrence's early life was not that of a source of inspiration, a muse; the help she gave him was essentially practical — criticising, discussing, supplying him with detailed notes and comments. For years her own literary ability was sunk in what she calls her 'co-operation' in Lawrence's work. On one of their very last meetings:

> We talked about his writing and he upbraided me for not making an effort to do something myself. He was so sure I could write if

I would try. 'If you had only two books out, I shouldn't care,' he said. I knew he was reproaching himself for having occupied my time with his own work.[25]

When Lawrence had first started to write what later became *The White Peacock*, in 1906, the idea had been that Jessie should start a novel at the same time. 'Lawrence now began to talk definitely of writing. He said he thought he should try a novel, and wanted me to try to write one too, so that we could compare notes.'[26] Jessie does not say why she did not produce anything herself, but she read through the first pages that Lawrence brought her, and from then on

> Lawrence was constantly bringing his writing to me, and I always had to tell him what I thought of it. He would ask whether the characters had developed, and whether the conversation was natural, if it was what people really would say.[27]

Lawrence wrote with Jessie and her opinion constantly in mind. Her taste had been to some extent formed by him, since she had received much of her informal education at his hands; and from being his pupil she became his critic. But she had a mind of her own and was never afraid to tell him when she disliked what he had done. Although she shared closely in the composition of *The White Peacock* — Lawrence wrote to her, 'I its creator, you its nurse'[28] — she seems at first to have provided mostly encouragement of a general kind. It was in the writing of *Sons and Lovers* that her co-operation became crucial.

Lawrence began writing *Paul Morel* (later *Sons and Lovers*) in the autumn of 1910, around the time that he broke his unofficial engagement to Jessie. He began the novel again early in 1911. Later that year he sent the entire manuscript — between half and two-thirds of the story — to Jessie, and asked her to tell him what she thought of it. Her opinion of it was not very high.

> The writing oppressed me with a sense of strain. It was extremely tired writing . . . The spontaneity that I had come to regard as the distinguishing feature of his writing was quite lacking. He was telling the story of his mother's married life, but the telling seemed to be at second hand, and lacked the living touch. I could not help feeling that his treatment of the theme was far behind the reality in vividness and dramatic strength.[29]

Jessie suggested that Lawrence should start again, and write straight from his own experience, telling things exactly as they had happened. Her motives were twofold. First, she simply thought that it would make a better novel; secondly, she felt that if Lawrence was forced to come face to face, in his writing, with the problem of his relationship with his mother and his traumatic involvement with herself, his psychosexual problems might be resolved. In other words, she saw the possibility that the writing might be therapeutic. 'It seemed to me that if he was able to treat the theme with strict integrity he would thereby walk into freedom, and cast off the trammelling past like an old skin.'[30] As if he had only been waiting for Jessie's permission to tell the story as it really happened — for there is no doubt that the writing of *Sons and Lovers* was indeed a therapeutic experience for Lawrence, although the issue was not what Jessie had hoped — he wrote back agreeing completely with her diagnosis and asking for her help. 'He ... asked me to write what I could remember of our early days, because, as he truthfully said, my recollection of those days was so much clearer than his. I agreed to do so, and began almost at once.'[31] In February 1912 Jessie gave him the notes she had written. He had broken his engagement to Louie Burrows, and he and Jessie were back, for a brief spell, on something like their old terms.

> Lawrence passed the manuscript on to me as he wrote it, a few sheets at a time, just as he had done with *The White Peacock*, only that this story was written with incomparably greater speed and intensity.
>
> The early pages delighted me. Here was all that spontaneous flow, the seemingly effortless translation of life that filled me with admiration.[32]

But Jessie's admiration turned to dismay as she read Lawrence's portrayal of herself as the frigid, spiritual Miriam. She felt betrayed by his depiction of their relationship, and 'the shock of *Sons and Lovers* gave the death-blow to our friendship'.[33] In spite of this final break, Lawrence still wanted to know what Jessie thought of the novel. She arranged a rendezvous at which she merely told him that she had put some notes in with the manuscript; this was almost their last meeting, for soon afterwards Lawrence went to Europe with Frieda. But the desperate need that Lawrence appears to have had for Jessie's approbation can be seen from the fact that he sent her the proofs of *Sons and Lovers* to read in the spring of 1913, an action which profoundly distressed her.³⁴

The picture that emerges is one of an almost obsessive need on Lawrence's part for Jessie's seal of approval. We would certainly not have the naturalistic *Sons and Lovers* that we have now, were it not for Jessie's prompting of Lawrence to confront his own experience as directly as possible. Some of her notes and comments on the work in progress (the 'Miriam Papers') are in the Humanities Research Center of the University of Texas. The papers consist of three manuscript sections in Jessie's hand (the recollections of incidents from their past that Lawrence requested); 23 pages of Lawrence's manuscript with Jessie's comments, including material eventually omitted from *Sons and Lovers*; and four pages of extra comment by Jessie. An account of the content of the 'Miriam Papers' is given in an appendix to Harry T. Moore's critical biography of Lawrence.³⁵ It is clear that some of the most vivid scenes in the novel derive from Jessie's reminiscences. Lawrence often takes sentences directly from her manuscript; some of the descriptions of nature, especially, go into *Sons and Lovers* almost exactly as Jessie wrote them. Moore has commented that 'her prose is lead, his quicksilver', and warned against overestimating her part in the novel's composition. 'She as a recorder gave him a sequence of remembered facts; he as an imaginative artist dramatically intensified them and made them into literature.'³⁶ But to ignore the part Jessie played is as misleading as to over emphasise it. The story of her involvement with Lawrence's literary work has an ironic ending. After Lawrence had left her she wrote an autobiographical novel, *Eunice Temple*, which she sent to him in 1913, possibly in a spirit of revenge (she later destroyed it). Years later she confessed that she thought she saw evidence of Lawrence's reading of it in *The Rainbow*.³⁷

Lawrence's second novel, *The Trespasser*, was based on a 'diary' of Helen Corke's which she wrote during the summer of 1909, describing the holiday she had taken with her lover, a music teacher, prior to his suicide. Helen makes it clear in her autobiography that the 'Freshwater Diary'³⁸ was a private and therapeutic piece of writing.

> During the autumn I have finished a brief, retrospective diary of the first week of August. The writing of this has been self-indulgence — the opportunity to live again those precious hours; to enshrine them in words. I have chosen the words, balanced the phrases, very carefully.³⁹

Lawrence helped Helen to come to terms with her grief at this difficult period of her life, and she agreed to show him her writing; he had already asked her to read the manuscript of *Nethermere* (*The White Peacock*) and give him her impressions. 'I give him the diary. There is a new urgency in his voice when he returns it. "What are you going to *do* with these prose poems?" he asks. I reply — nothing.'[40] Lawrence became fascinated by the story of Helen and 'Siegmund', and finally asked whether he could use Helen's record of her experiences as the basis for a novel of his own.

> He returns to the subject of my Freshwater diary later — comes with the request that he may take it and expand its theme — use the poems as basis for a more comprehensive rendering of the story. He will bring me the work as it grows; nothing shall stand with which I am not in agreement. It shall be a finished study in full accordance with my suggestions.[41]

Helen, admiring what she had seen of Lawrence's writing and trusting to his tact, consented. She declined to scrutinise the manuscript in detail as the work progressed, but Lawrence brought each chapter to her as it was completed, and she does not appear to have objected at any point to his treatment. On the contrary, she wrote that 'the intuition it shows, the rare symbolism, fill me with wonder'.[42]

Lawrence clearly identified with the Siegmund of the story; Helen felt that it was due to his ability to put himself in Siegmund's place that the novel was successful. Indeed, he began to feel a mounting sexual attraction for her during its composition, a feeling which Helen, despite her fondness for him, did not return. The novel does not therefore simply expand Helen's impressionistic diary into a structured narrative. It gives Siegmund's thoughts and feelings throughout, and in fact we have a fuller psychological picture of Siegmund in the finished novel than we have of Helena, whose character seems ultimately to have mystified Lawrence. *The Trespasser* follows fairly closely the events described in Helen's diary, and whole sentences of her prose are incorporated unchanged. Apart from filling out the narrative, inventing dialogue, and so on, Lawrence's major innovation was to include the actual scene of Siegmund's suicide and to place the whole story in a wider context, giving, for example, a picture of his unhappy marriage, without which the suicide would seem less credible. Lawrence also includes a self-portrait, a young man called Cecil Byrne who comforts Helena and seems, at the end of the novel, to have won her love — not merely, one feels, to provide a traditional happy ending, but as an act of wish-fulfilment on Lawrence's part; a desire, perhaps subconscious, to impose his version of their relationship on Helen, just as in the writing of *Sons and Lovers* one feels that he was trying to do the same with Jessie. Lawrence of course justified his version on aesthetic grounds in both cases, and in both cases the women concerned later wrote their own accounts (Helen's novel *Neutral Ground* was published in 1933). Lawrence wrote to Helen:

> As you remember saying yourself, the Saga is a work of fiction on a frame of actual experience. It is my presentation, and therefore necessarily false sometimes to your view. The necessity is not that our two views should coincide, but that the work should be a work of art.[43]

Helen did not in fact see the final revision of the manuscript before it went into print. Originally she and Lawrence had agreed that the novel should not be published for five years, although Lawrence tried to place it with a publisher. However, his illness during the winter of 1911-12 and his subsequent decision to give up teaching left him short of money, and he asked Helen for permission to publish, which she gave him. The book was brought out in May 1912, and Lawrence sent Helen a copy from Germany. She wished he had not revised it, but on the whole she was not displeased with the result.

> When the book arrives I open it with mingled exaltation and dread. Why, if there has been no sacrifice of its essential truth to his Moloch of technique and form, did he not send me the revised manuscript as promised? But indeed the work remains substantially the same — the eroticism of one imaginary scene has been heightened; there are several interpolations of imaginary dialogue — and I miss a fine piece of symbolism — yet it is still the record, faithful enough, of Lawrence's exploration into the territory of H.B.M.'s experience.[44]

It would seem, then, that Lawrence's collaboration with Helen Corke was a relatively happy one. Having given Lawrence permission to use her diary she let him have a free hand, and her remarkable powers of detachment, which had already helped her to come to terms with the tragedy of her lover's suicide, appear to have prevented her from feeling that her own identity was too closely implicated in the character of Helena.

Lawrence revised *Sons and Lovers* in Italy during the second half of 1912, and seems to have enlisted Frieda's help in the rewriting. She says, 'I lived and suffered that book, and wrote bits of it when he would ask me: "What do you think my mother felt like then?" '[45] Frieda also told Mabel Dodge Luhan that she had written pages of *Sons and Lovers*; on another occasion she claimed to have written 'little female bits'.[46] It would be hard to find two women more dissimilar than Lydia Lawrence and Frieda Weekley, but Lawrence believed he had found, in Frieda, an epitome of universal womanhood through whom he had access to a generalised female experience. There are few other instances of her contributing in a direct way to Lawrence's work, although she was often a trenchant critic; but her claim to a place in Lawrence's writing is of course at once larger and more diffuse than any of the other women he knew.[47] There are close textual similarities between Frieda's memoirs and parts of *The Rainbow*; but Frieda wrote her memoirs after Lawrence's death, and it is impossible to tell to what extent they are themselves influenced by his literary treatment of incidents in her life. The question of Frieda's 'influence' on Lawrence — critics still have not tired of debating whether she was a supreme source of inspiration or a fatal mistake — is part of a more general biographical issue which there is not space to discuss here. But one detail is interesting: Frieda was never the patient amanuensis. 'He didn't expect me to type,' she wrote. 'I hated it. Poor as we were he never expected me to do it.'[48]

In 1922 Lawrence stayed briefly in a guest house in Darlington, Australia, run by a woman called Mollie Skinner. She was trained as a midwife, but had made a name for herself as a writer in a small way, and had published a record of her experiences as a nurse during the First World War. Lawrence read and enjoyed this, and asked her why she didn't write something about the early settlers in Australia. She was thus encouraged to show him the manuscript of a novel she had been writing called *Black Swans*, which he found a 'wild MS, climbing the mountain of impossibilities and improbabilities by leaps and bounds'.

> Oh, and the ponderous manuscript, tangled, and simply crepitating with type-writer's mistakes, which I read with despair in that house in Western Australia. Such possibilities! And such impossibilities.
>
> But the possibilities touched with magic. Always hovering over the borderline where probability merges into magic: then tumbling, like a bird gone too far out to sea, flopping and splashing into the wrong element, to drown soggily.[49]

Lawrence advised her, much as Jessie Chambers had advised him over ten years before, to write from her own experience. He suggested her brother Jack as a central character. Mollie Skinner enumerated her objections — she had no time, she had received no proper education, she knew nothing about style, her family disapproved of her writing and it would 'bring hell's fire' on her head if she based a novel on the lives of those she knew intimately. 'Although I was a good midwife,' she writes, 'I was unsure of myself as a writer.'[50] Lawrence countered her objections and told her to send him what she wrote; he would see about getting it published.

In 1923, in New Mexico, Lawrence received from Mollie Skinner the manuscript of the story he had urged her to write, which she had called *The House of Ellis*. Lawrence thought it better than *Black Swans*, but still 'tangled, gasping, and forever going under in the sea of incoherence'.[51] He was reluctant to raise her hopes, but the story seemed to him to have potential. He wrote to her:

> I have read *The House of Ellis* carefully — such good stuff, but without unity or harmony. I'm afraid as it stands you'd never find a publisher. Yet I hate to think of it all wasted. I like the quality of so much of it. But you have no constructive power. — If you like I will take it and re-cast it, and make a book of it. In which case we should have to appear as collaborators, or assume a pseudonym. — If you give me a free hand, I'll see if I can't make a complete book out of it.[52]

Mollie Skinner consented, and Lawrence 'wrote the whole book over again, from start to finish, putting in and leaving out, yet keeping the main substance of Miss Skinner's work'.[53] He worked swiftly, and was soon writing to warn her that the ending would have to be 'different, a good deal different,' and that he had made 'a rather daring development, psychologically'.[54]

It is difficult to estimate how much of *The Boy in the Bush* (as *The House of Ellis* became) is Lawrence's, and how much is Mollie Skinner's.[55] The style is distinctively Lawrence's throughout, and it seems that, as he rewrote, he must have welded his own idiosyncratic technique onto Mollie Skinner's narrative. The 'daring psychological development' would seem to be the transformation of the central character into a Lawrentian hero with decided views on such subjects as polygamy. In January 1924 Lawrence sent the typescript of *The Boy in the Bush* to Mollie Skinner. She did not object to his rewriting except at the end.

> When at last I brought myself to read the script, I found that Lawrence had twisted its tail, even adding a new character. I saw why Mittie [her sister] had fumed, although I myself gloried in the touches Lawrence had given it. I was dismayed, however, that he had altered the construction and pulled it out of focus towards the end. Jack, the hero I had drawn, would never have ridden a snorting stallion amongst the old shellbacks, intent on seducing their daughters.[56]

One imagines that the novel's emphasis on 'manhood', which places it with *Aaron's Rod*, *Kangaroo*, *The Plumed Serpent* and the other works of the early 1920s, was not part of Mollie Skinner's original design. However, she merely wrote to Lawrence 'thanking him for making such a fine job of it generally, but begging him to twist the tail back into place'.[57] Lawrence reluctantly asked his publisher to make the changes she asked for if possible,[58] but her wishes were not respected and *The Boy in the Bush* was published with Lawrence's controversial ending.

Lawrence's letters to Mollie Skinner express regret that the publicity material for the book had capitalised on his fame and left her in the background; they also reveal that the division of the royalties was executed with scrupulous fairness. Lawrence undertook no further collaborations with Mollie Skinner, although in 1928 he sent her detailed comments and suggestions on another manuscript which was never published,[59] and we know that he tacitly edited articles of hers which appeared in the *Adelphi*.[60] It is difficult to see why this literary friendship, conducted almost entirely by post, endured so long. It may be significant that there was obviously no sexual tension in the relationship. Mollie Skinner, who was already well into middle age when she met Lawrence, and who had a full and busy life of her own outside her writing, was simply grateful for the help and encouragement of an established author. Her conviction that she was his inferior in education and literary know-how seems to have made her willing to accept his rewriting of her work almost without protest.

After leaving Australia in 1922 Lawrence went to New Mexico at the invitation of Mabel Dodge Luhan, a wealthy American who had gone to live there. The issue of Lawrence's collaboration with women, indeed the whole question of his relationship with women, here begins to shade off into farce. Mabel candidly admits that she *willed* Lawrence to come to Taos, and a reading of her three-volume autobiography and its continuation in *Lorenzo in Taos*[61] goes quite some way towards explaining Lawrence's bitter attacks on dominating women and the vicious female 'will'. Mabel's only redeeming grace is her candour. She openly admitted being a 'predatory woman'[62] and spent most of her life trying to find men through whom she could exercise power. 'A woman cannot and never will be able to do anything without the man, who releases her into creative action,'[63] she wrote and elsewhere stated that 'the function of the male principle is to give impetus to the feminine life'.[64] In search of the right man through whom to achieve 'a sense of fruitfulness and activity vicariously',[65] she married four times and had numerous lovers, espousing *en route* a variety of more or less radical causes.

Mabel wanted Lawrence to take her life and imbue it with significance through a magic process of art. 'I wanted Lawrence to understand things for me. To take *my* experience, *my* material, *my* Taos, and to formulate it all into a magnificent creation.'[66] Her wish was temporarily granted. Lawrence rose to the bait and asked her if she would work on a novel with him.

> He said he wanted to write an American novel that would express the life, the spirit, of America and he wanted to write it around me — my life from the time I left New York to come out to New Mexico; my life, from civilization to the bright, strange world of Taos; my renunciation of the sick old world of art and artists, for the pristine valley and the upland Indian lakes. I was thrilled at the thought of this. To work with him, to give him myself — Tony — Taos — every part of the untold and undefined experience that lay in me like a shining, indigestible jewel that I was unable either to assimilate or to spew out! I had been holding on to it for so long, solitary and aware, but helplessly inexpressive!
>
> Of course it was for this that I had called him across the world.[67]

The collaboration never progressed very far. Lawrence's first words on joining Mabel the morning they were supposed to start 'work' were, 'I don't know how Frieda's going to feel about this.'[68] Frieda in fact insisted that work on this novel should be done in their house and not in Mabel's, and her shrewd honesty in recognising Mabel as a sexual rival is refreshing after Mabel's mystical mumbo-jumbo. The project fizzled out:

> How could I talk to Lawrence and tell him my feelings and experiences with *Frieda* in the room? . . . Then and there I saw it was over,

and I should never have the opportunity to get at him, and give him what I thought he needed or have, myself, the chance to unload my accumulation of power.[69]

The opening pages of this abortive work have been published under the title 'The Wilful Woman'.[70] There also remains a letter of Lawrence's asking Mabel for notes about her experiences, which he has broken down into a list of ten sections, and for a short story of hers which he speaks of incorporating.[71]

It may be said that in Mabel Lawrence met his match, and didn't much like what he found. On the other hand, her obsessive desire to submit and be used must have been flattering. She is unique among the women who were involved with Lawrence's writing in her *conscious* desire for him to take her life and turn it into a significant fiction; and her case points up the difficulty of passing a simplistic judgement and casting Lawrence as the villain of the piece. It is fairer to say that the mythology of woman's experience as the raw material of art and man's intelligence as its shaping force is shared by both sexes and not necessarily imposed upon women against their will — although one can, of course, find examples where it *is* a bitterly resented imposition, as in the case of Zelda Fitzgerald.[72]

One further example may suffice as an indication of Lawrence's method. Catherine Carswell recalls that, between visits to New Mexico, Lawrence called to ask her whether she would be one of the people to go back there with him and form a new type of community. She carefully explained that she did not feel able to leave her husband and young child. She and Lawrence had been good, though unobtrusive, friends for years, and had always taken a keen mutual interest in each other's work (she was a novelist and critic). To soften the blow of her refusal she began to tell him of an idea she had in mind for a new novel. Lawrence was interested in her theme and suggested that they should collaborate. 'I like that story of yours so much, Catherine, that I've written out a little sketch of how I think it might go. Then, if you like the idea, we might collaborate in the novel.'[73] Lawrence's synopsis of this unwritten novel is printed by Catherine Carswell in her biography of him, and reprinted in Harry T. Moore's *The Priest of Love*.[74] Lawrence apparently suggested that Catherine Carswell should 'do the beginning and get the woman character going' and he would 'go on and fill in the man'.[75] She says that she began to work upon the beginning, decided that she was not up to it, and lost heart: she does not intimate whether it was Lawrence's taking over of her idea that disheartened her, or whether she herself had planned a quite different treatment of the theme; but the novel remained unwritten.

I would not wish to overload the phenomenon I have been describing with a significance which it does not really merit. It must be said that the extent to which people other than the author are involved in the process of writing a novel (or anything else) is widely underestimated; such involvement frequently goes much further and much deeper than we imagine. The Romantic concept of the artist has tended to blind us to this, as to other conditions of literary production, with the result that the spectrum which runs from plagiarism to genuine collaboration has not received much study. But the pattern I have pointed to in Lawrence's life and work, which can be found in varying degrees in many other authors, seems significant, particularly when the author in question is known for his special relationship to femininity or his skill in depicting the female psyche.

Catherine Carswell's anecdote, and Lawrence's attitude towards Frieda, seem to endorse the theory that he sought help from women in order to verify his portrayal of female psychology. But in many cases, women provide him with narrative structure or plot, and with descriptions, often of nature, rather than with psychological insight. In *Sons and Lovers* and *The Trespasser* it is the small, incidental details of landscape which Lawrence tends to pick out from the material supplied to him by Jessie Chambers and Helen Corke; one is inevitably reminded of the way in which Wordsworth built on the foundation of Dorothy's observations. The characterisations of Miriam in the first novel and Helena in the second owe little or nothing to material supplied by their originals; in Jessie Chambers's case, Lawrence deliberately chose to disregard the information she gave him about her own feelings and attitudes at various crucial points in their relationship. In the writing of *The Boy in the Bush*, Lawrence took Mollie Skinner's narrative and her knowledge of the Australian landscape and atmosphere, and used it as the background against which to set the development of a Lawrentian hero.

Frequently, Lawrence seems to appropriate not just material but the creative instinct itself. On more than one occasion, by taking over the idea almost before she has formulated it, his intervention seems to stop a woman writing something herself, as with Helen Corke's poem and Catherine Carswell's novel. But then it is also noticeable that several of the women whom Lawrence knew betray an attitude towards writing very different from his — it is for them a private, almost therapeutic affair; often, as in Helen Corke's case, it takes the form of a diary written with no thought of publication. Lawrence is of course himself an intensely personal writer, and one who believed that the artist 'sheds his sicknesses' in books; yet his urge is always to turn the experience into fictive form, and to *publish*.

Notes

1. Letter to Arthur McLeod, 2 June 1914. *Letters*, vol. 2, p. 181.
2. Review of F. Scott Fitzgerald's *The Beautiful and Damned*, New York *Tribune*, 2 April 1922, cited in Nancy Milford, *Zelda Fitzgerald: A Biography* (Bodley Head, London, 1970), p. 89.
3. See Charles Rossman, '*The Boy in the Bush* in the Lawrence Canon' in Robert B. Partlow and Harry T. Moore (eds.), *D.H. Lawrence: The Man Who Lived* (Southern Illinois University Press, Carbondale, 1980), pp. 185-94.
4. Harry T. Moore, *The Priest of Love* (revised edition, Heinemann, London, 1974), p. 51.
5. 'E.T.', *D.H. Lawrence: A Personal Record* (Jonathan Cape, London, 1935), p. 116.
6. *Poems*, pp. 98-9.
7. Helen's original poem is not extant but the incident that inspired it is recorded in *In Our Infancy* (Cambridge University Press, Cambridge, 1975), pp. 195-6.
8. Moore, *The Priest of Love*, p. 102.
9. See George J. Zytaruk (ed.), *The Quest for Rananim: D.H. Lawrence's Letters to S.S. Koteliansky* (McGill-Queen's University Press, Montreal, 1970).
10. Daniel Defoe, *Moll Flanders* (3rd edition, London, 1722), pp. i-ii.
11. See Ellen Moers, *Literary Women* (W.H. Allen, London, 1977), p. 116.
12. Carolyn G. Heilbrun, *Towards Androgyny: Aspects of Male and Female in Literature* (Victor Gollancz, London, 1973), p. 49.
13. Ibid., pp. 93-4.
14. Rosalind Miles, *The Fiction of Sex: Themes and Functions of Sex Difference in the Modern Novel* (Vision Press, London, 1974), p. 49.
15. Kate Millett, *Sexual Politics* (Hart-Davis, London, 1971), p. 239.
16. Letter to Louie Burrows, September 1906. *Letters*, vol. 1, p. 30.
17. Ibid., pp. 29-30.
18. Letter to Louie Burrows, 29 October 1906. Ibid., p. 32.
19. Letter to Louie Burrows, 30 June 1909. Ibid., p. 130.
20. Letter to Louie Burrows, 27 July 1909. Ibid., p. 132.
21. Letter to Louie Burrows, 19 August 1909. Ibid., p. 136.
22. Letter to Louie Burrows, 27 July 1909. Ibid., p. 133.
23. Letters to Louie Burrows, 20 November 1909 and 9 March 1910. Ibid., pp. 144 and 156.
24. 'E.T.', *D.H. Lawrence: A Personal Record*, p. 141.
25. Ibid., p. 200.
26. Ibid., p. 103.
27. Ibid., p. 115.
28. Ibid., p. 189.
29. Ibid., p. 190.
30. Ibid., p. 192.
31. Ibid., p. 193.
32. Ibid., pp. 197-8.

33. Ibid., pp. 202-3.
34. See George J. Zytaruk (ed.), 'The Collected Letters of Jessie Chambers', *D.H. Lawrence Review*, vol. 12, nos. 1 and 2 (1979), pp. 26-8.
35. Harry T. Moore, 'The Genesis of *Sons and Lovers* (as revealed in the Miriam Papers)': Appendix D of *The Life and Works of D.H. Lawrence* (Allen and Unwin, London, 1951), pp. 365-87.
36. Moore, *The Priest of Love*, p. 52.
37. Emile Delavenay, *D.H. Lawrence: L'Homme et la Genèse de son Œuvre* (2 vols., Librarie C. Klincksieck, Paris, 1969), vol. 2, p. 709.
38. Printed as an appendix to Corke, *In Our Infancy* and also to the Cambridge edition of *The Trespasser*.
39. Corke, *In Our Infancy*, p. 176.
40. Ibid., p. 177.
41. Ibid., p. 178.
42. Ibid., p. 180.
43. Letter to Helen Corke, 1 February 1912. *Letters*, vol. 1, p. 359. (*The Trespasser* was originally called 'The Saga of Siegmund'.)
44. Corke, *In Our Infancy*, p. 216.
45. Frieda Lawrence, *Not I, But the Wind...* (Heinemann, London, 1935), p. 52.
46. Frieda Lawrence, *The Memoirs and Correspondence*, ed. E.W. Tedlock (Heinemann, London, 1961), p. 186.
47. See Anne Smith, 'A New Adam and a New Eve – Lawrence and Women: A Biographical Overview' in Anne Smith (ed.), *Lawrence and Women* (Vision Press, London, 1978), pp. 9-48.
48. Frieda Lawrence, *Not I, But The Wind...*, p. 80.
49. 'Preface to *Black Swans*', *Phoenix II*, p. 294.
50. M.L. Skinner, *The Fifth Sparrow* (Angus and Robertson, London, 1973), p. 115.
51. 'Preface to *Black Swans*', *Phoenix II*, p. 294.
52. Letter to Mollie Skinner, 2 September 1923. *Collected Letters*, p. 751.
53. 'Preface to *Black Swans*', *Phoenix II*, p. 295.
54. Letter to Mollie Skinner, 1 November 1923. *Collected Letters*, p. 760.
55. See Rossman, '*The Boy in the Bush* in the Lawrence Canon'.
56. Skinner, *The Fifth Sparrow*, p. 128.
57. Ibid., p. 129.
58. Martin Secker (ed.), *Letters from D.H. Lawrence to Martin Secker 1911-1930* (privately published, Bridgefoot Iver, 1970), p. 56.
59. Skinner, *The Fifth Sparrow*, p. 168.
60. Letter to John Middleton Murry, 12 December 1925. *Collected Letters*, p. 869.
61. Mabel Dodge Luhan, *Intimate Memories*: vol. 1, *Background* (Martin Secker, London, 1933); vol. 2, *European Experiences* (Harcourt, Brace, New York, 1935); vol. 3, *Movers and Shakers* (Harcourt, Brace, New York, 1936); and *Lorenzo in Taos* (Martin Secker, London, 1933).
62. Luhan, *European Experiences*, p. 390.
63. Luhan, *Lorenzo in Taos*, p. 241.
64. Luhan, *European Experiences*, p. 7.
65. Luhan, *Lorenzo in Taos*, p. 77.
66. Ibid., p. 77.
67. Ibid., p. 59.
68. Ibid., p. 67.
69. Ibid., p. 70.
70. *The Princess and Other Stories*, pp. 15-21.
71. Letter to Mabel Dodge Luhan, Autumn 1922. *Collected Letters*, p. 724.
72. Lawrence's use of women's writing may be compared with the way in

which Scott Fitzgerald drew on the diaries and letters of his wife Zelda, and collaborated with her on stories and articles. Fitzgerald often transferred large sections of Zelda's writing more or less verbatim into his work. When George Nathan, editor of *The Smart Set*, made Zelda an offer for her diaries, Scott said that he could not permit him to publish them because 'he had gained a lot of inspiration from them and wanted to use parts of them in his own novels and short stories' (Milford, *Zelda Fitzgerald: A Biography*, p. 71). Several stories published under Scott's name were in fact Zelda's work, such as 'Our Own Movie Queen', of which Scott noted: 'Two thirds written by Zelda. Only my climax and revision' (ibid., p. 102). Zelda received no credit for the story, but Scott split the $1,000 payment for it with her, just as Lawrence had split his rather more modest fee for 'Goose Fair' with Louie Burrows. Of 'A Millionaire's Girl' Scott wrote that it 'appeared under my name but actually I had nothing to do with it except for suggesting a theme and working on the proof of the completed manuscript' (ibid., p. 150.). Sometimes articles or stories written by Zelda alone were attributed to both Fitzgerlads, often at the insistence of the magazine in which they were published. Scott admitted that 'this same cooperation extends to other material gathered ... under our joint names, though often when published in that fashion I had nothing to do with the thing from start to finish except supplying my name' (ibid.). He also revised work by Zelda to 'get it into shape'. A friend noted Scott's remark that 'Z would do six articles for *College Humor*, that he would go over them and fix them up and that the articles would be signed with both their names' (ibid., p. 149). Like Lawrence, Fitzgerald was an intensely autobiographical novelist, and he clearly regarded the shared fabric of his tempestuous life with Zelda as his exclusive source-material. When Zelda herself began to put some of the experiences of her life, including her relationship with Scott, into fiction (in her autobiographical novel *Save Me The Waltz*), Scott was furious and accused her of plagiarism, forgetting his own ransacking of her diaries and letters. Scott's hysterical efforts to prevent Zelda writing, his refusal to admit that her life might be a source of literary inspiration for her as well as for him, seem to have played a crucial part in her mental collapse. Compared to Fitzgerald's exhaustive draining of one woman, Lawrence's promiscuity in this respect seems almost like a gesture of kindness.

73. Catherine Carswell, *The Savage Pilgrimage* (Martin Secker, London, 1932), p. 211.

74. Ibid., pp. 211-14; Moore, *The Priest of Love*, pp. 382-4.

75. Carswell, *The Savage Pilgrimage*, p. 211.

BIBLIOGRAPHY

Works by D.H. Lawrence

The following Penguin editions have been used (date of first publication in brackets):

The White Peacock (1911)
Sons and Lovers (1913), ed. Keith Sagar
The Prussian Officer and Other Stories (1914)
The Rainbow (1915), ed. John Worthen
Twilight in Italy (1916)
Women in Love (1920), ed. Charles L. Ross
Aaron's Rod (1922)
England, My England (1922)
Fantasia of the Unconscious (USA 1922, UK 1923) and *Psychoanalysis and the Unconscious* (USA 1921, UK 1923)
Kangaroo (1923)
Three Novellas (*The Ladybird, The Fox, The Captain's Doll*) (1923)
Studies in Classic American Literature (1923)
The Boy in the Bush (with M.L. Skinner) (1924)
St Mawr (1925) and *The Virgin and the Gipsy* (1930)
The Plumed Serpent (1926)
Mornings in Mexico (1927) and *Etruscan Places* (1932)
Lady Chatterley's Lover (1928)
A Propos of Lady Chatterley's Lover and Other Essays (1930)
The Mortal Coil and Other Stories (contains stories not collected in Lawrence's lifetime)
The Princess and Other Stories (contains stories not collected in Lawrence's lifetime)
The First Lady Chatterley (USA 1944, UK 1972)
John Thomas and Lady Jane (1972)

Other editions:

The Trespasser (1912), ed. Elizabeth Mansfield (Cambridge University Press, Cambridge, 1981)
The Lost Girl (1920), ed. John Worthen (Cambridge University Press, Cambridge, 1981)

Boulton, James T. (gen. ed.). *The Letters of D.H. Lawrence* vol. 1, ed. James T. Boulton (Cambridge University Press, Cambridge 1979); vol. 2, ed. George J. Zytaruk and James T. Boulton (1981)

McDonald, Edward D. (ed.). *Phoenix: The Posthumous Papers of D.H. Lawrence* (Heinemann, London, 1936)

Moore, Harry T. (ed.). *The Collected Letters of D.H. Lawrence* (2 vols., Heinemann, London, 1962)

Pinto, Vivian de Sola and Warren Roberts (eds.). *The Complete Poems of D.H. Lawrence* (2 vols., Heinemann, London, 1964)

Roberts, Warren and Harry T. Moore (eds.). *Phoenix II: Uncollected, Unpublished and Other Prose Works by D.H. Lawrence* (Heinemann, London, 1968)

Secker, Martin (ed.). *Letters from D.H. Lawrence to Martin Secker 1911-1930* (privately published, Bridgefoot Iver, 1970)

Zytaruk, George J. (ed.). *The Quest for Rananim: D.H. Lawrence's Letters to S.S. Koteliansky* (McGill-Queen's University Press, Montreal, 1970)

Other Works

Adam, Ruth. *A Woman's Place 1910-1975* (Chatto and Windus, London, 1975)

Adams, Parveen. 'Representation and Sexuality', *m/f*, no. 1 (1978)

Allen, Grant. *The Woman Who Did* (John Lane, London, 1895)

Banks, J.A. and Olive. *Feminism and Family Planning in Victorian England* (Liverpool University Press, Liverpool, 1964)

Beauvoir, Simone de. *The Second Sex*, tr. H.M. Parshley (Jonathan Cape, London, 1953)

Blanchard, Lydia. 'Love and Power: A Reconsideration of Sexual Politics in D.H. Lawrence', *Modern Fiction Studies*, vol. 21, no. 3 (1975)

Blast, no. 1 (1914)

Box, Muriel (ed.). *The Trial of Marie Stopes* (Femina Books, London, 1967)

Brittain, Vera. *Testament of Youth* (Victor Gollancz, London, 1933)

Brome, Vincent. *Freud and his Early Circle: The Struggles of Psycho-Analysis* (Heinemann, London, 1967)

Burroughs, Edgar Rice. *Tarzan of the Apes* (Methuen, London, 1917)

Busst, A.J.L. 'The Image of the Androgyne in the Nineteenth Century' in Ian Fletcher (ed.), *Romantic Mythologies* (Routledge and Kegan Paul, London, 1967)

Carlyle, Thomas. *Latter-Day Pamphlets* (Chapman and Hall, London, 1850)

Carpenter, Edward. *Love's Coming-of-Age: A Series of Papers on the Relations of the Sexes* (Labour Press, Manchester, 1896)

────── *The Intermediate Sex: A Study of some Transitional Types of Men and Women* (Swan Sonnenschein, London, 1908)

────── *The Drama of Love and Death: A Study of Human Evolution and Transfiguration* (George Allen, London, 1912)

────── *Intermediate Types Among Primitive Folk: A Study in Social Evolution* (George Allen, London, 1914)

Carswell, Catherine. *The Savage Pilgrimage: A Narrative of D.H. Lawrence* (Martin Secker, London, 1932)

Chambers, Jessie: see 'E.T.'

────── 'Collected Letters', ed. George J. Zytaruk, *D.H. Lawrence Review*, vol. 12, nos. 1 and 2 (1979)

Corke, Helen. *Neutral Ground* (Arthur Barker, London, 1933)

────── *D.H. Lawrence: The Croydon Years* (University of Texas Press, Austin, 1965)

────── *In Our Infancy – An Autobiography: Part I, 1882-1912* (Cambridge University Press, Cambridge, 1975)

Daleski, H.M. *The Forked Flame: A Study of D.H. Lawrence* (Faber and Faber, London, 1965)

Dangerfield, George. *The Strange Death of Liberal England* (Constable, London, 1936)

Darroch, Robert. *D.H. Lawrence in Australia* (Macmillan, Melbourne, 1981)

Davies, Margaret Llewelyn (ed.). *Life As We Have Known It, by Co-Operative Working Women* (Hogarth Press, London, 1931)

Defoe, Daniel. *Moll Flanders* (3rd edition, London, 1722)

Delavenay, Emile. 'Sur an Exemplaire de Schopenhauer annoté par D.H. Lawrence', *Revue Anglo-Americaine*, vol. 13, no. 3 (1936)

────── *D.H. Lawrence: L'Homme et la Genèse de son Œuvre: les Années de Formation, 1885-1919* (2 vols., Librarie C. Klincksieck, Paris, 1969)

────── *D.H. Lawrence and Edward Carpenter: A Study in Edwardian Transition* (Heinemann, London, 1971)

Edge, John. 'D.H. Lawrence and the Theme of Comradeship', *Southern Review*, vol. 9, no. 1 (1976)

The Egoist. 1914-19

Ellis, Havelock. 'Thomas Hardy's Novels', *Westminster Review*, 1 April 1883

—— *The New Spirit* (George Bell, London, 1890)
—— *Man and Woman: A Study of Human Secondary Sexual Characters* (Walter Scott, London, 1894)
—— 'Concerning *Jude the Obscure*', *Savoy*, October 1896
—— 'The Objects of Marriage', *Birth Control Review*, June 1917
—— 'The Love Rights of Woman', *Birth Control Review*, June 1918
'E.T.' (Jessie Chambers). *D.H. Lawrence: A Personal Record* (Jonathan Cape, London, 1935)
Farr, Florence. *Modern Woman: Her Intentions* (Frank Palmer, London, 1910)
Ford, Ford Madox. *Mightier Than The Sword* (Allen and Unwin, London, 1938)
Ford, George H. *Double Measure: A Study of the Novels and Stories of D.H. Lawrence* (Holt, Rinehart and Winston, New York, 1965)
The *Freewoman*. 1911-12
Fussell, Paul. *The Great War and Modern Memory* (Oxford University Press, London, 1975)
Gates, G. Evelyn (ed.). *The Woman's Year Book 1923-1924* (Women Publishers, London, 1924)
Gibbs, Philip. *Since Then* (Heinemann, London, 1930)
Gollancz, Victor (ed.). *The Making of Women: Oxford Essays in Feminism* (Allen and Unwin, London, 1917)
Goode, John. 'D.H. Lawrence' in Bernard Bergonzi (ed.), *The Twentieth Century* (History of Literature in the English Language, vol. 7, Barrie and Jenkins, London, 1970)
Gomme, A.H. 'Jessie Chambers and Miriam Leivers' in A.H. Gomme (ed.), *D.H. Lawrence: A Critical Study of the Major Novels and Other Writings* (Harvester, Hassocks, 1978)
Gosse, Edmund. 'Mr. Hardy's New Novel', *Cosmopolis*, vol. 1, no. 1 (1896)
Gray, Cecil. *Peter Warlock: A Memoir of Philip Heseltine* (Jonathan Cape, London, 1934)
Green, Eleanor H. 'Schopenhauer and D.H. Lawrence on Sex and Love', *D.H. Lawrence Review*, vol. 8, no. 3 (1975)
Green, Martin. *The Von Richthofen Sisters: The Triumphant and the Tragic Modes of Love* (Weidenfeld and Nicolson, London, 1974)
Haldane, J.B.S. *Daedalus, or Science and the Future* (Kegan Paul, Trench, Trubner, London, 1924)
Hall, Ruth. *Marie Stopes: A Biography* (André Deutsch, London, 1977)
Hardy, Thomas. *Jude the Obscure* (revised edition, Macmillan, London, 1912)

―――― *Collected Letters*, vol. 2, ed. Richard Little Purdy and Michael Millgate (Oxford University Press, Oxford, 1980)

Heilbrun, Carolyn G. *Towards Androgyny: Aspects of Male and Female in Literature* (Victor Gollancz, London, 1973)

Heilman, Robert B. 'Hardy's Sue Bridehead', *Nineteenth Century Fiction*, vol. 20, no. 4 (1966)

Heywood, Christopher. 'D.H. Lawrence's *The Lost Girl* and its Antecedents by George Moore and Arnold Bennett', *English Studies*, vol. 47, no. 2 (1966)

Hoffman, Frederick. *Freudianism and the Literary Mind* (Louisiana State University Press, Baton Rouge, 1945)

Hull, E.M. *The Sheik* (Eveleigh Nash, London, 1919)

James, William. *The Order of Release: The Story of John Ruskin, Effie Gray and John Everett Millais* (John Murray, London, 1947)

Kinkead-Weekes, Mark. 'The Marble and the Statue: The Exploratory Imagination of D.H. Lawrence' in Maynard Mack and Ian Gregor (eds.), *Imagined Worlds: Essays on some English Novels and Novelists in Honour of John Butt* (Methuen, London, 1968)

Lacan, Jacques. *The Language of the Self: The Function of Language in Psychoanalysis*, tr. A. Wilden (Johns Hopkins Press, Baltimore, 1968)

Lawrence, Frieda. *Not I, But The Wind . . .* (Heinemann, London, 1935)

―――― *The Memoirs and Correspondence*, ed. E.W. Tedlock (Heinemann, London, 1961)

Leavis, Q.D. *Fiction and the Reading Public* (Chatto and Windus, London, 1932)

Lemons, J. Stanley. *The Woman Citizen: Social Feminism in the 1920s* (University of Illinois Press, Urbana, 1973)

Lewis, Jane. 'Beyond Suffrage: English Feminism in the 1920s', *Maryland Historian*, vol. 6, no. 1 (1975)

Low, Barbara. *Psycho-Analysis: A Brief Account of the Freudian Theory* (Allen and Unwin, London, 1920)

Ludovici, A.M. *Woman: A Vindication* (Constable, London, 1923)

―――― *Lysistrata, or Woman's Future and Future Woman* (Kegan Paul, Trench, Trubner, London, 1925)

―――― *Man: An Indictment* (Constable, London, 1927)

Luhan, Mabel Dodge. *Lorenzo in Taos* (Martin Secker, London, 1933)

―――― *Intimate Memories*: vol. 1, *Background* (Martin Secker, London, 1933); vol. 2, *European Experiences* (Harcourt, Brace, New York, 1935); vol. 3, *Movers and Shakers* (Harcourt, Brace, New York,

1936)

Lynd, Robert. 'The Downfall' (review of *The Rainbow*), *Daily News and Leader*, 5 October 1915

Martz, Louis L. 'Portrait of Miriam: A Study in the Design of *Sons and Lovers*' in Maynard Mack and Ian Gregor (eds.), *Imagined Worlds: Essays on some English Novels and Novelists in Honour of John Butt* (Methuen, London, 1968)

Marwick, Arthur. *Women at War 1914–1918* (Fontana, London, 1977)

Meyer, Jeffrey. 'D.H. Lawrence and Homosexuality' in Stephen Spender (ed.), *D.H. Lawrence: Novelist, Poet, Prophet* (Weidenfeld and Nicolson, London, 1973)

—— *Painting and the Novel* (Manchester University Press, Manchester, 1975)

Miles, Rosalind. *The Fiction of Sex: Themes and Functions of Sex Difference in the Modern Novel* (Vision Press, London, 1974)

Milford, Nancy. *Zelda Fitzgerald: A Biography* (Bodley Head, London, 1970)

Millett, Kate. *Sexual Politics* (Hart-Davis, London, 1971)

Mitchell, David. *Women on the Warpath: The Story of the Women of the First World War* (Jonathan Cape, London, 1966)

Mitchell, Juliet. *Psychoanalysis and Feminism* (Allen Lane, London, 1974)

Mitchison, Naomi. *Comments on Birth Control* (Criterion Miscellany no. 12, Faber and Faber, London, 1930)

Moers, Ellen. *Literary Women* (W.H. Allen, London, 1977)

Moore, Harry T. *The Life and Works of D.H. Lawrence* (Allen and Unwin, London, 1951)

—— *The Priest of Love: A Life of D.H. Lawrence* (revised edition, Heinemann, London, 1974)

Murry, John Middleton. *Son of Woman: The Story of D.H. Lawrence* (Jonathan Cape, London, 1931)

Myers, Neil. 'Lawrence and the War', *Criticism*, vol. 4, no. 1 (1962)

Nehls, Edward (ed.). *D.H. Lawrence: A Composite Bibliography* (3 vols., University of Wisconsin Press, Madison, 1957–9)

Neville-Rolfe, Mrs. 'The Changing Moral Standard', *The Nineteenth Century and After*, vol. 84 (1918)

New Freewoman. 1913

Nin, Anaïs. *D.H. Lawrence: An Unprofessional Study* (Edward W. Titus, Paris, 1932)

Oliphant, Mrs. 'The Anti-Marriage League', *Blackwood's Magazine*, January 1896

Pankhurst, Christabel. *The Great Scourge and How to End it* (WSPU, London, 1913)

Raeburn, Antonia. *The Militant Suffragettes* (Michael Joseph, London, 1973)

Rathbone, Eleanor. Presidential address at the annual council meeting of the National Union of Societies for Equal Citizenship, *Woman's Leader*, 13 March 1925

Robinson, Paul. *The Modernization of Sex* (Paul Elek, London, 1976)

Rossman, Charles. ' "You are the Call and I am the Answer": D.H. Lawrence and Women', *D.H. Lawrence Review*, vol. 8, no. 3 (1975)

—— 'The Boy in the Bush in the Lawrence Canon' in Robert B. Partlow and Harry T. Moore (eds.), *D.H. Lawrence: The Man Who Lived* (Southern Illinois University Press, Carbondale, 1980)

Rover, Constance. *Love, Morals and the Feminists* (Routledge and Kegan Paul, London, 1970)

Rowbotham, Sheila. *Women, Resistance and Revolution* (Allen Lane, London, 1972)

—— *Hidden from History* (Pluto Press, London, 1973)

—— *A New World for Women: Stella Browne — Socialist Feminist* (Pluto Press, London, 1977)

—— and Jeffrey Weeks. *Socialism and the New Life: The Personal and Sexual Politics of Edward Carpenter and Havelock Ellis* (Pluto Press, London, 1977)

Russell, Dora. *Hypatia, or Woman and Knowledge* (Kegan Paul, Trench, Trubner, London, 1925)

Sagar, Keith. *D.H. Lawrence: A Calendar of his Works* (Manchester University Press, Manchester, 1979)

Schopenhauer, Arthur. *Essays*, tr. Mrs Rudolf Dircks (Walter Scott, London, 1897)

Schreiner, Olive. *Woman and Labour* (Fisher Unwin, London, 1911)

Skinner, M.L. *The Fifth Sparrow* (Angus and Robertson, London, 1973)

Smith, Anne (ed.). *Lawrence and Women* (Vision Press, London, 1978)

Smith, Timothy d'Arch. *Love in Earnest: Some Notes on the Lives and Writings of English 'Uranian' Poets from 1889 to 1930* (Routledge and Kegan Paul, London, 1970)

Stopes, Marie. *Married Love* (Putnam, London, 1918)

—— *Marriage in My Time* (Rich and Cowan, London, 1935)

Swigg, Richard. *Lawrence, Hardy and American Literature* (Oxford University Press, London, 1972)

Taylor, Rachel Annand. *The Hours of Fiammetta: A Sonnet Sequence*

(Elkin Matthews, London, 1910)

Trilling, Lionel. 'Tickets, Please' in *Prefaces to the Experience of Literature* (Oxford University Press, Oxford, 1981)

Tyrrell, R.Y. 'Jude the Obscure', *Fortnightly Review*, 1 June 1896

Ussher, R. *Neo-Malthusianism* (Gibbings, London, 1898)

Vanggaard, Thorkil. *Phallós: A Symbol and its History in the Male World* (Jonathan Cape, London, 1972)

Vivas, Eliseo. *D.H. Lawrence: The Failure and the Triumph of Art* (Northwestern University Press, Evanston, 1960)

Votes for Women. 1907-10

Ward, A.C. *The 1920s: Literature and Ideas in the Post-War Decade* (Methuen, London, 1930)

Weininger, Otto. *Sex and Character* (Heinemann, London, 1906)

Wells, H.G. *Ann Veronica: A Modern Love Story* (Fisher Unwin, London, 1909)

Woodeson, John. *Mark Gertler: Biography of a Painter, 1891-1939* (Sidgwick and Jackson, London, 1972)

Zytaruk, George J. 'The Phallic Vision: D.H. Lawrence and V.V. Rozanov', *Comparative Literature Studies*, vol. 4, no. 3 (1967)

INDEX

Aaron's Rod 37, 105–18 *passim*, 157
Allen, Grant, *The Woman Who Did* 22, 46
A Propos of Lady Chatterley's Lover 137
Arnold, Matthew 24, 94
Asquith, Lady Cynthia 65, 93

Beardsley, Aubrey 46, 51, 52
Beauvoir, Simone de, *The Second Sex* 13, 131, 132
Bennett, Arnold, *Anna of the Five Towns* 74
Blanchard, Lydia 13–14
Blast 25
Bondfield, Margaret 20, 30–1, 44n57
Boy in the Bush, The 143, 156–7, 160
Brittain, Vera 105
Burroughs, Edgar Rice, *Tarzan of the Apes* 125
Burrows, Louie 21, 49, 143, 144, 147–9

Campbell, Gordon 65
'Captain's Doll, The' 71, 111
Carlyle, Thomas 130
Carpenter, Edward 17, 20, 24, 81–91 *passim*
    Drama of Love and Death, The 86
    Intermediate Sex, The 38, 40, 86–7
    Intermediate Types Among Primitive Folk 58–9
    Love's Coming-of-Age 84, 89–90
Carswell, Catherine 143, 144, 159–60
Chambers, Jessie ('E.T.') 20, 49, 57, 147
    involvement in writing of *The White Peacock* and *Sons and Lovers* 143, 144, 149–52, 160
'Coldness in Love' 144
contraception 82, 97n23, 102–3
Co-operative Women's Guild 19, 26–7

Corke, Helen 21, 49, 51, 87, 144–5
    involvement in writing of *The Trespasser* 143, 152–4, 160
    Neutral Ground 54–5, 154

Daleski, H.M., *The Forked Flame* 15, 129
Dax, Alice 19, 20, 28
Defoe Daniel, *Moll Flanders* 145–6
Delavenay, Emile, *D.H. Lawrence and Edward Carpenter* 38, 83
Dell, Ethel M. 123, 125
Despard, Mrs Charlotte 20, 46–7

Eder, David 91
'Education of the People' 93
Ellis, Havelock 17, 81–91 *passim*
Etruscan Places 131–2

Fantasia of the Unconscious 15, 91–6, 104, 105–8, 115, 127
Farr, Florence 87
First Lady Chatterley, The 135–6
Fitzgerald, Scott and Zelda, 159, 160, 162–3n72
Fliess, Wilhelm 86, 97–8n28
Ford, Ford Madox 20, 24, 130
Forster, E.M. 147
    Where Angels Fear to Tread 79n42
'Fox, The' 66, 70–3, 77, 111
'Fragment of Stained Glass, A' 148
Freewoman see *New Freewoman*
Freudianism 82, 91–2, 94, 122, 130–1, 132

Gertler, Mark 132
Gibbs, Philip, *Since Then* 100, 103–4
Gissing, George, *The Odd Women* 33, 74–5
Goats and Compasses 37
Goode, John 27
'Goose Fair' 149
Gosse, Edmund 48
Gross, Otto 92

Haldane, J.B.S. 103
Hardy, Thomas

Jude the Obscure 48-9, 59, 83
Tess of the d'Urbervilles 83
Heilbrun, Carolyn G., *Towards Androgyny* 147
Heilman, Robert B. 48-9
Heseltine, Philip 83
Heywood, Christopher 74
Hoffman, Frederick, *Freudianism and the Literary Mind* 91-2
homosexuality 37-41, 85-6
Hopkin, Sallie 19
Hueffer, Ford Madox *see* Ford, Ford Madox
Hull, E.M., *The Sheik* 17, 123-8 *passim*

James, Henry 147
The Bostonians 22, 33, 40
John Thomas and Lady Jane 136-7, 140
Jung, Carl 92

Kangaroo 37, 105, 108-15 *passim*, 157
Koteliansky, S.S. 145

Lacan, Jacques 132-3
'Ladybird, The' 71
Lady Chatterley's Lover 78
 and 'phallic consciousness' 130-40 *passim*
 relationship to popular novels of the 1920s 125-6
Lambert, Cecily 70-1
Lawrence, Frieda 66, 151, 158
 and Freudianism 91-2
 involvement in Lawrence's writing 143, 155, 160
Lawrence, Mrs Lydia 19, 27, 155
Leavis, Q.D., *Fiction and the Reading Public* 103, 123
Lost Girl, The 73-8
Low, Barbara 24, 91, 98n51
Ludovici, A.M. 104-5, 119-20n29
Luhan, Mabel Dodge 143, 155, 157-9

Mansfield, Katherine 66, 92, 93
Men's League for Woman Suffrage 19
Meredith, Hugh 66
Meyers, Jeffrey 41
Miles, Rosalind, *The Fiction of Sex* 147
Millett, Kate, *Sexual Politics* 13, 132, 147
 on *Lady Chatterley's Lover* 131, 136
 on *Sons and Lovers* 29, 36
Mitchell, Juliet, *Psychoanalysis and Feminism* 132
Mitchison, Naomi 102
'Modern Lover, A' 57-8
Moers, Ellen, *Literary Women* 131
Monk, Violet 70-1
'Monkey Nuts' 66, 69-70, 71
Monroe, Harriet 134
Moore, George 51
 A Mummer's Wife 74, 76
Moore, Harry T., *The Priest of Love* 143, 152, 159
Morrell, Lady Ottoline 58, 59
'Mother and Daughter' 127-8
Murry, John Middleton 13, 92
Myers, Neil 64

National Union of Societies for Equal Citizenship 102
National Union of Women's Suffrage Societies 19
New Age 20-1
New Feminism 101-2, 106
New Freewoman (formerly *Freewoman*) 23-4, 43n17, 81, 84, 97n7
Nin, Anaïs, *D.H. Lawrence: An Unprofessional Study* 13
novel, development of 145-7
'Novel, The' 133

Oliphant, Mrs 48

Pankhurst
 Christabel 47, 63
 Mrs Emmeline 19, 63
 Sylvia 46
 in Eastwood 20
phallus 128-34
 in *John Thomas and Lady Jane* 136-7, 140
 in *Lady Chatterley's Lover* 137-40
 in *The First Lady Chatterley* 135-6
 in *The Plumed Serpent* 134-5, 138
Plumed Serpent, The 111, 113-17, 138, 157
 and male comradeship 37, 105,

108–9
and 'phallic consciousness' 134–5
relationship to popular novels of the 1920s 125
'Prelude, A' 148
Pre-Raphaelitism 46–53 *passim*, 56–8
'Princess, The' 126–7
Psychoanalysis and the Unconscious 91

Rainbow, The 16, 76, 91, 130, 144
   and *Eunice Temple* (Jessie Chambers) 152
   and Frieda Lawrence 155
   and homosexuality 37–41
   and suffragism 41–2
   and the 'erotic movement' 92
Rathbone, Eleanor 101
'Real Thing, The' 108
Richardson, Samuel 146
'Rose of All the World' 85
Rowbotham, Sheila, *Hidden from History* 63, 122–3
Royden, Maude 99, 122
Ruskin, John 142
Russell, Bertrand 39, 66
Russell, Dora 102

St Mawr 117–19, 126–7
Schopenhauer, Arthur 51, 82, 83, 87, 98n33
Schreiner, Olive
   The Story of an African Farm 54
   Woman and Labour 21, 41, 47
'Shades of Spring, The' 58
Skinner, Mollie 143, 144, 155–7, 160
Social Feminism *see* New Feminism
Sons and Lovers
   and the 'spiritual woman' 56–7
   and women's rights 26–37
   Frieda Lawrence's involvement in composition 155
   Jessie Chamber's involvement in composition 143, 149, 150–2, 154, 160
Stopes, Marie, *Married Love* 102, 122
Studies in Classic American Literature 108, 111
Study of Thomas Hardy 15, 65, 92, 95
   and *Jude the Obscure* 59
   and suffragism 24
   as expression of Lawrence's early sexual theory 82–91
'Surgery for the Novel – Or A Bomb' 128

Taylor, Rachel Annand 49–50
'Tickets, Please' 63, 66, 67–9, 71, 72
Trespasser, The 53–4, 130, 143, 152–4, 160
Trilling, Lionel 67
Twilight in Italy 90

Vivas, Eliseo, *D.H. Lawrence: The Failure and Triumph of Art* 112, 131
Von Richthofen, Else 91, 92
Votes for Women 19, 46

war
   and sexual freedom 64, 102–3
   and the 'woman surplus' 75
   and women's employment 63–4, 99–100
   effect on men 100
   Lawrence's reaction to 64–7
Weininger, Otto, *Sex and Character* 82–91 *passim*, 96n6
Wells, H.G. 75, 118
   Ann Veronica 22–3, 74
White Peacock, The 153
   and homosexuality 37, 38
   and Pre-Raphaelitism 51–3
   and women's rights 25–6
   Jessie Chamber's involvement in composition 144, 150, 151
'White Stocking, The' 148
'Wilful Woman, The' 159
'Witch à la Mode, The' 55–6
Women in Love 39, 41, 92, 123
   and homosexuality 37, 118
   and the 'spiritual woman' 59–60
   and the war 16, 65
Women's Army Auxiliary Corps (WAAC) 64
Women's Freedom League 47
Women's Guild *see* Co-operative Women's Guild
Women's Land Army 64, 70, 72
Women's League 26, 51, 82
Women's Social and Political Union (WSPU) 19, 32, 40, 42, 46, 81
Wordsworth, William and Dorothy 160